MOSEBY
CONFIDENTIAL

BY THE SAME AUTHOR

At the End of the Street in the Shadow:
Orson Welles and the City (2016)

MOSEBY CONFIDENTIAL

Arthur Penn's *Night Moves*
and the Rise of Neo-Noir

Matthew Asprey Gear

Copyright © 2019 Matthew Asprey Gear

All rights reserved.

ISBN-10: 0-9863770-8-2

ISBN-13: 978-0-9863770-8-2

Library of Congress
Catalog No: 2019932297

Cover design/formatting: Keith Carlson

Author photo: Jace Davies

Back cover photo: TCD/Prod.DB / Alamy Stock Photo

First edition

Jorvik Press

5331 SW Macadam Ave., Ste. 258-424,
Portland OR 97239

JorvikPress.com

About the Author

Matthew Asprey Gear is the author of *At the End of the Street in the Shadow: Orson Welles and the City.* His writings on film and literature have appeared in the *Los Angeles Review of Books, Senses of Cinema,* and *Bright Lights Film Journal,* and his fiction in many publications, including *Crime Factory.* He lives in Edinburgh, Scotland.

Acknowledgments

I'm grateful to the following individuals who helped in various ways during the writing of this book: Noel King, Susan Clark, Jennifer Warren, Bonnie Bruckheimer, Matthew Penn, Liz Sharp, Dan Sharp, Mufidah Kassalias, François Thomas, Adrian Martin, Lukas Kendall, Andie Childs, Derrick Farnell, and Jack London. I also want to thank my mother, Julie Asprey.

I especially want to thank Nat Segaloff, author of the foundational biography *Arthur Penn: American Director* (2011), who was extremely helpful and generous throughout the writing of this project. His interviews with Alan Sharp, Melanie Griffith, and Robert M. Sherman have been essential research materials.

Matthew Asprey Gear
Edinburgh Central Library, December 2018

*For Noel King –
last of the independents*

> *"Knights had no meaning in this game.
> It wasn't a game for knights."*
>
> Raymond Chandler, *The Big Sleep*[1]

Contents

Prologue: The Edge of America 1

1. The Baltimore Bench (1922-1972) 7

2. An End of Wishing (1972-1973) 39

3. The First Six Feet (Summer-Autumn, 1973) 65

4. The Dark Tower (Autumn-Winter, 1973) 77

5. Night Moves (1974) 111

6. The Shark Tank (1975) 125

Coda: Second Prize in a Fight 135

Appendix: Film Credits 141

Notes and References 145

Index 159

Prologue:
The Edge of America

The sixties were ending and Alan Sharp, a young Scottish novelist in America, found his muse on the frontier. By then everything seemed to be falling apart. Hopes and certainties had evaporated. Consensus was fractured. It was the bloody season of political assassinations. Thomas McGuane, another wild and libidinous young writer, would begin a Key West novel with an appropriately sweeping summation of despair: "Nobody knows, from sea to shining sea, why we are having all this trouble with our Republic."[2] Alan Sharp, no stranger to despair, also found his way to the sparkling waters, the fetid swamps, the heavy air of the Florida Keys.

It was a pilgrimage for a writer who loved John Huston's *Key Largo* (1948) and, adopted at birth, had once imagined Humphrey Bogart as his long-lost father.[3] Sharp recognised the mythical value of the Keys in the collective imagination. It was a last stop before Mexico, that fantasy destination for escaping renegades and the more irredeemable dropouts of the counter-culture. But in Sharp's outsider grasp of American myth, such characters never really escaped.[4] Like the coast of California or the Rio Grande, the Keys were the edge of America – a place of spectacular culmination or of resignation and decay.

During his visit in the spring of 1968, one stop on an epic cross-country road trip, Sharp encountered a sardonic drifter. "I met this girl working in a bar in the Keys and she fascinated me," he remembered. "She lived on the shore. She had a free spirit."[5] Her name was Paula and she was romantically involved with an unlikely married man. Sharp later elaborated:

> *She was from Malone up in New York State. I said, "What's your deal here?" I basically asked her why she's with this guy, who was a kind of conch, fishery guy. And not a studly dude. She said, "Well, he's the only guy I've met down here who doesn't disimprove when he drinks. And everybody drinks." At that moment Paula became my heroine.*[6]

After the '68 road trip Sharp went back to London where he established himself in the movie business as a screenwriter. He returned on several occasions to explore the US and Mexico. Finally, circa 1971, as his films began to reach cinemas, he relocated his young family to Hollywood. Throughout this upheaval he was unable to forget Paula. With her in mind, he began sketching two screenplays.

One would become *Night Moves*. Sharp figured it would begin as a private detective pastiche, following the conventional pathways of the genre, but then the detective's investigation would dissipate. Along the way he might fall into a love affair in the Keys with a tough woman like Paula. Together they would run off with the loot. The romance would "end in disaster" and the mystery would remain unsolved. The film would reflect what Sharp defined as a new American consciousness at the close of the sixties, "a recognition that the world is more complex than what it was believed to be and that there are things that just cannot be solved."[7]

In early 1973 a draft of the screenplay reached Arthur Penn, whose *Bonnie & Clyde* (1967) had made him one of the leading renegade directors of what would be called the New Hollywood. But Penn hadn't made a feature film in several years. Exhausted by the making of his radical anti-western *Little Big Man* (1970) and a shocked bystander at the 1972 Munich Olympics massacre, Penn was in a state of disillusion. He remembered:

> *I went through a really difficult period after* Little Big Man. *[...] Actually... I lost my identity. I just gave up on things. I lost myself. For three years I stopped doing what really made me happy and what I really wanted to do. [...] When I decided I wanted to direct again, I just chose the first script to hand. Impulsively and without really thinking about it I just told myself I was going to direct Alan Sharp's screenplay.*[8]

The making of *Night Moves* is the story of the collaboration of two artists of starkly different sensibilities – Alan Sharp the hopeless fatalist, Arthur Penn the agitating progressive. Each was just beginning to descend from his peak of cultural relevance. Sharp and Penn came together in 1973 to make a dark film about an America bereft of answers. Everything seemed in place for a triumph. Finally, in careers plagued by compromise, there was both an adequate budget and artistic freedom. Gene Hackman's performance would expertly particularise an archetype fracturing before our eyes – the knightly private detective unable to solve his case, the macho American male desperate for certainty but lost at sea. But neither Penn nor Sharp was satisfied with the resulting movie and they disagreed over its final form. After a long delay, Warner Brothers cut its losses and dumped *Night Moves* into cinemas with a half-hearted publicity campaign. The movie's reviews were mixed and it failed to make a profit in the summer of 1975. That season was dominated by Steven Spielberg's *Jaws*, which provided Hollywood with a new and super-profitable model of film production.

And yet *Night Moves* has gone on to be recognised as one of the defining films of the 1970s, both as a profound human drama and as an enduring evocation of the zeitgeist. This Technicolor neo-noir, along with Robert Altman's *The Long Goodbye* (1973) and Roman Polanski's *Chinatown* (1974), reinvented and redeemed the private detective movie. A reactionary, nostalgia-crazed culture industry had tried to neuter the genre, reduce it to a repertoire of clichéd gestures. This trio of pictures re-asserted film noir as an ideal cinematic language to explore the darkness at the heart of America.

1. The Baltimore Bench
(1922-1972)

The trio of key collaborators on *Night Moves* were all of a sensitive breed of men – the yearning sons of absent fathers. Gene Hackman's father drove off one day with a casual wave to his thirteen-year-old boy and never returned.[9] Alan Sharp, adopted as a baby to sternly Calvinist parents, never knew his birth father, a Dundee communist.[10] For Arthur Penn, the fatherly absence was not only long periods of separation, but also the emotional distance of the taciturn male.

Penn was born in Philadelphia in 1922. The marriage of his parents, Lithuanian Jewish immigrants, did not last. "I'm a child of divorce who was torn between two separate families when I was growing up," he said.[11] Raised by his mother, Penn did not reunite with his father, a watchmaker, until his teens. By then the man was terminally ill with bladder cancer. He died in 1941. Penn recalled, "I never knew much about my father. He was a withdrawn man, and I was a withdrawn adolescent. We didn't make enough contact to amount to a hill of beans. I regret that deeply, and wish I'd known more about the man."[12]

As a young boy, Penn hadn't been much of a moviegoer. One frightening picture made him hide under his seat and refuse to come out. After that trauma, he avoided the experience for years.[13] But he eventually became interested in theatre. Penn fought in the Second World War in the US Army Infantry and saw action in the Battle of the Bulge. He also produced theatre for the Soldiers' Shows unit. After the war he stayed on in Europe. He went to Nuremberg and watched the war crimes trials of Herman Göring and other architects of the genocide of his people. This glimpse of evil would stay with Penn.

Back in the USA, he studied philosophy and psychology through the GI Bill at Black Mountain College in North Carolina, a thriving community of intellectuals and avant-garde artists. Then Penn returned to Europe to study Italian in Perugia. By the age of thirty he was travelled, experienced and educated. In 1955 he married Peggy Maurer. They would raise two children and remain together until his death in 2010.[14]

While his older brother, Irving, became a world-famous photographer, Arthur Penn made his career in television, theatre and film. He possessed an enduring agility that equipped him for the physical challenges of directing ("the man was a mountain goat," recalled producer Robert M. Sherman[15]). He was modest, generous and widely liked. In the 1950s Penn worked for NBC in New York and Los Angeles, working his way up to directing live plays in the "Golden Age of Television." Before the total ubiquity of TV in American homes, programming was culturally aspirational. Live television drama was a writers' medium, closer in its practices to theatre than film, and attracted leading dramatists. The tight production schedules and rapid turnover honed the skills of a generation of writers, directors, actors and technicians. Scheduled for prime time, television plays were broadcast live to huge audiences. "It was rather like flying test planes," recalled Penn. "You'd go on the air at eight o'clock and bang! Across the country!"[16]

In the same period Penn worked successfully as a theatre director. Invited to join the Actors Studio in New York, he would come to specialise in directing that generation of youthful actors who expressed post-war sensitivity and rebellion – Paul Newman, Warren Beatty, Dustin Hoffman, Jack Nicholson, and the greatest of them all, Marlon Brando.

Some of the most successful television plays were remade by Hollywood film studios as features, often in collaboration with independent production companies, a gambit that led to the award-winning triumphs *Marty* (Delbert Mann, 1955), *Twelve Angry Men* (Sidney Lumet, 1957), *Requiem for a Heavyweight* (Ralph Nelson, 1962) and *Days of Wine and Roses* (Blake Edwards, 1962). And it wasn't only the material that travelled from one medium to the other; TV directors like Lumet, John Frankenheimer and Franklin J. Schaffner now began to make movies. This new school brought socially progressive themes back to Hollywood after the purge of leftists by the House Unamerican Activities Committee. Arthur Penn also seized the day and directed *The Left-Handed Gun* (1958), a feature adaptation of Gore Vidal's 1955 teleplay *The Death of Billy the Kid*. It was one of the earliest starring roles for Paul Newman.

Paul Newman as Billy the Kid in *The Left Handed Gun* (1957)

At its worst the western had perpetuated, in the form of popular entertainment, a celebratory myth of American imperialism that justified the genocide of Native Americans. But with its potential for visual grandeur and spectacular action, political allegory and moral ambiguity, the western had become a favoured cinematic terrain for ambitious, morally serious filmmakers. Robert Warshow's *Partisan Review* essay, "The Westerner" had made a pitch for the genre's critical worthiness in 1954. John Ford had just produced *The Searchers* (1956) and Anthony Mann was coming to the end of a decade-long run of masterful westerns, both with and without actor James Stewart. Yet the "revisionist" western, which sought to demolish the genre's founding myths, had not yet really arrived. Arthur Penn was an early instigator of that revisionism. He thought of *The Left-Handed Gun* as an "anti-western" and blamed the film's indifferent critical reception in America on his irreverent approach. "Apparently the western is one of those sacred and untouchable genres," he said in 1976.[17]

One of the disruptive aspects of *The Left-Handed Gun* was its atypical characters. Penn said, "It's insane that young people in westerns aren't portrayed as being cantankerous, giddy kids who do all kinds of crazy personal things with sexual overtones."[18] Newman's Billy is a beautiful, sensitive, rebellious young man in the style of Marlon Brando in *The Wild One* (1953) and James Dean in *Rebel Without a Cause* (1955). The vaguely homoerotic carousing of Billy's gang was probably a consequence of Vidal's lingering influence.[19]

Penn wasn't allowed to complete *The Left-Handed Gun* to his satisfaction. Warner Brothers insisted a staff editor cut the film without Penn's oversight. This was the first of Penn's many skirmishes over artistic independence in Hollywood. He was never comfortable working within the industry. He disliked the expense and scale of American movie-making, as well as the technicians' unions which, in his view, prevented established directors from choosing to work independently.

He came to envy the freedom enjoyed in Europe, particularly by the French New Wave – their low budgets, small non-union crews, and freedom to "grab a camera and go out with three or four friends and make a film." He was frustrated that Hollywood's "notion of a film has to be committed to paper [which] has to be filtered through a series of descending intelligences until finally we arrive at a point where someone will write a check for a film that his son or daughter will want to see."[20]

Although Penn never committed his total energy to a career in the movies – he maintained a successful parallel career on Broadway – he worked on a series of varied and thematically daring projects through the 1960s. His fortunes were mixed. He made an award-winning film version of William Gibson's *The Miracle Worker* (1962), which he had initially directed as a TV play (1957) and then as a hit Broadway show (1959). Riding high, the following year he was fired from *The Train*, a project he had instigated with United Artists, just days into shooting at the behest of its leading actor, Burt Lancaster (Penn was replaced by John Frankenheimer). Penn then made two pictures for Columbia: a low-budget experiment called *Mickey One* (1965), and a star-studded melodrama about southern bigotry, *The Chase* (1966). In the latter film Marlon Brando played a liberal sheriff battling to uphold the law in a town of vigilante racists. Again, Penn was barred from supervising post-production; producer Sam Spiegel had the movie edited in England while Penn was committed to directing a play in New York.

Yet Penn kept making movies and was able to obtain creative control. He collaborated for the first time with master editor Dede Allen on *Bonnie and Clyde* (1967), a great and controversial success. This time the "cantankerous, giddy kids" are Depression-era bandits who become folk heroes for robbing the same banks that have ravaged the poor folk of Texas. Penn doesn't easily grant their Robin Hood credentials. We witness the naive and ignorant Bonnie and Clyde stumble into that role and then attempt to live up to the legend. Penn also doesn't glorify the characters' violence, which is depicted with unprecedented explicitness.

Faye Dunaway, Denver Pyle, and Warren Beatty in *Bonnie and Clyde* (1967)

Bonnie is a self-involved sociopath who, out of boredom, attaches herself to Clyde, an anti-establishment daredevil troubled by his capacity for killing. These were an unprecedented pair of heroes for Hollywood cinema, a flaunting of the rules of sympathetic protagonists. Penn bet on the glamour, charisma, and sex appeal of Faye Dunaway and Warren Beatty to transcend the challenges of audience identification. The horrific violence of the characters' execution by the police makes martyrs of the pair, yet the film doesn't argue for the virtue of their rampage. *Bonnie and Clyde* works as a metaphor: energetic beautiful youth fighting a losing battle against mature authority; Billy the Kid killed by Pat Garrett.

. . .

Alan Sharp came from a different world – provincial Scotland – but he also came to know the ache of a fatherless son. Born in 1934, he was adopted as an infant by an austere working-class couple, Joe and Meg Sharp, who lived on the Clyde River in Greenock. His deeply religious adopted father would terrify young Alan with the prospect of Hell. "If I bumped into the fucking table I used to say 'Sorry, God,'" Sharp remembered. "When I was a boy you didn't whistle on a Sunday, food was cooked on a Saturday to minimize disturbance of the Sabbath, you didn't break sticks or play football (the fact that Catholics did after twelve o'clock Mass seemed to my father the clearest indication of the Satanic nature of the Church of Rome) and you went endlessly to Kirk, or the mission or the Salvation Army or whatever your variant was."[21]

Greenock had seven picture theatres.[22] Sharp loved American movies, particularly westerns and Humphrey Bogart films, and internalised their myths. He remembered, "When your life was a tenements-and-back-lots-and-broken-glass-sparkling-in-the-sun kind of deal, you wanted a way in which the feelings that belonged to you, and which were looking for a larger landscape, could be expressed."[23]

Sharp was unaware of his adoption until his teens. The discovery gave him a welcome sense of independence from the Sharps. "He was delighted because he could barely relate to them," remembers Sharp's third wife Liz. "They were very simple people. He could hardly believe he was their son because his mind was so active."[24] Now Sharp felt free to invent his true parents. He said he chose "Humphrey Bogart as my father and Katharine Hepburn as my mother" – surely inspired by their joint appearance in John Huston's *The African Queen* (1951). Bogart was, Sharp later remembered, "the most reasonable and humane" movie hero of the era.[25] But Sharp wouldn't be able to leave the mystery of his origins there.

He left school at fourteen and worked in Greenock's shipyards. Reaching maturity, he was conscripted into the army. He went to Glasgow University and, after a failed first marriage that produced two children, moved to London and remarried.[26] He wrote plays for broadcast on the BBC, including the radio drama *The Long-Distance Piano Player* (1962; later a TV play, 1970) and the original teleplays *Funny Noises with their Mouths* (1963), starring up-and-comers Michael Caine and Ian McShane, and *A Knight in Tarnished Armour* (1965).

Curly-haired and leonine, bursting with energy and charisma, Sharp described himself in the sixties as "pathologically promiscuous."[27] He lived through a long period of "anarchic emotional and relational chaos."[28] Sharp fathered another four children to three women, including the novelist Beryl Bainbridge, in the second half of the 1960s.[29] Around 1968 he married for a third time, now to Liz, one of Bainbridge's friends from Liverpool. He and Liz had one infant son and a daughter on the way.

Liz Sharp found Alan to be "a very interesting person with a great sense of humour," but she reflects:

He had a big issue around women. Not seducing them so much – well, I guess it's all seduction – but he had to make them feel wonderful, whoever they were. [...] He wasn't really preoccupied with sex. He was preoccupied with being the centre of everybody's universe. He was a bit of a compulsive liar. [...] He was quite clever at having affairs, but at the same time it wasn't all hunky dory. It was a quite difficult relationship. No, not difficult. Bloody hard.

In his early adulthood Sharp had sought his roots. He'd learned that he had been born out of wedlock in the town of Alyth, the result of a promiscuous man's affair with his wife's friend. He would eventually track down his birth mother, now living alone, as well as a number of half-siblings, but by now his biological father, a communist from Dundee named Peter Craig, was dead.[30] According to Liz Sharp, Alan's father's romantic entanglements had been complicated. "It seemed to be the way Alan wanted his life to be. He wanted me to embrace his lovers and become their friends and almost live as one big commune. But that was not on the cards for me."

In this period Sharp completed two novels set mostly in Greenock. *A Green Tree in Gedde* (1965) and *The Wind Shifts* (1967) reimagine the romantic lives, thwarted dreams, and incestuous secrets of his hometown. Modest and self-critical, Sharp later described himself as a "turgid, purple-prose writer."[31] It is difficult to disagree. Despite believable characters – mostly tormented men, restless and in crisis – and a palpably chilly Scottish gloom, the narrative momentum often bogs in swamps of impressionistic prose, especially in the sex scenes. In a typical example a woman gives her lover "no outcome from the crutch close morticing join at the delirial vulva" until, "twitching in gorspasm [*sic.*]," he ejaculates "inth by inth [*sic.*]" a "normous [*sic.*] load, leaden molten rising outblow" that is last seen "shoaling upwards towards her welcoming interiors."[32]

Nevertheless, Sharp's turgid purple prose wasn't a commercial hindrance. Penguin Books had won the right to publish the unexpurgated *Lady Chatterley's Lover* in the United Kingdom in 1960, censorship barriers were breached, and the market was open to this type of sexually-focused but ostensibly literary fiction. Sharp's novels were well-reviewed and big sellers in paperback. He was translated and published internationally. In 1965 he'd gone to the US to promote his first novel.[33]

When Walker & Co. in New York published the sequel in late March of 1968, Sharp went back to America with Liz and their infant son. Sharp made an appearance at the book launch in a Greenwich Village cafe[34] and was interviewed for a widely-syndicated newspaper article. Wearing "a corduroy suit of matching shade," the thirty-four-year-old spoke confidently of how "yesterday's heroes... possessed a mystique valid for their day but now passé for us. Mine will share the preoccupations and relationships of our time – heroes able to live, to love, and to do."[35]

With his promotional duties completed, Sharp bought a second-hand Chevy II Nova and set out on an epic road trip with his wife, son, and the painter Peter Swan. "He loved endless car journeys," remembers Liz Sharp with a laugh. "He got a lot out of it. He could drive non-stop for days. It was hell as a mother with a young kid, because he didn't want to stop. We had to beg him to stop to eat!"

The landscapes of American cinema had allowed Sharp's imagination to transcend the provincial Greenock of his youth. Now he would visit the actual places he'd only ever seen in the movies. The itinerary would include the Florida Keys, a "sentimental journey" to a mythical place Sharp identified with Bogart and *Key Largo*.[36] It probably didn't matter to him that the film had been made almost entirely at Warner Brothers Studios in Hollywood.

John Huston's film had been another iteration of an emblematic Bogart hero – the jaded veteran who must be persuaded to join a new cause against evil. Following on from *Casablanca* (1942) and *To Have and Have Not* (1944), *Key Largo* dramatised the Bogart hero's switch from disillusionment to heroism when he agrees to take on a gangster. Sharp's fantasy father had now been dead more than a decade and in the meantime he'd become an American icon. Sharp was not uncritical in his assessment of Bogart's heroic relevance, but nevertheless observed that he "seems more valid now than in any of his previous phases... People like his cool, his hardness, his cynicism which is not total but which is an instrument... [they] think his performances are a reasonable way of behaving in the face of the world."[37]

Emphasising his perspective as a Scottish outsider exploring America, Sharp wrote a few articles for the *Los Angeles Times* to help pay for the trip. He could not have picked a more tumultuous season to take the nation's pulse.

Sharp was driving through the south on April 4 when Martin Luther King was assassinated in Memphis, Tennessee.[38] That night Robert F. Kennedy, campaigning in the Democratic primaries for the Presidential nomination, announced King's death at a rally in an African-American neighbourhood in Indianapolis. "In this difficult time for the United States," Kennedy said, "it's perhaps well to ask what kind of a nation we are and what direction we want to move in."[39] He encouraged love, wisdom, and compassion in America. But the year's violence would only increase.

As a result of the King assassination, the Academy Awards, scheduled for April 8, was postponed for two days. Best Picture went to *In the Heat of the Night*, Norman Jewison's film about southern racial intolerance. *Bonnie and Clyde* had been nominated for ten awards and won two, but Arthur Penn didn't attend the ceremony.[40]

During this spring of American discontent, the Sharps holed up for an extended stay in the Florida Keys. There they met the sardonic, free-spirited woman named Paula. She was no beauty. Liz Sharp recalls:

She was a hard-nosed little woman who was very much alone and was having an affair with a man who was married to a bossy sort of lady. They had boats and did excursions into the water where you could look through a glass-bottom. This affair wasn't with the wife's approval, but it was bizarre. We'd go evenings for dinners and this couple, the man and Paula, would dance about the room. Clearly she was intimate with the man but the wife seemed unaware of it. But not concerned. It was a very odd business.

Paula confided to Sharp her reason for accepting an unattractive lover: he was the only man around whose mood improved when he got drunk in that community of heavy drinkers. Paula, Sharp recognised, was an American archetype: the kind of "slightly shop-soiled, self-respecting" woman who never expects things to turn out well.[41] Sharp wanted to write that type of character. When she finally turned up onscreen, in a decidedly more glamorous incarnation, Paula would ask Sharp's protagonist the one question for which everybody should have had a ready answer:

"Where were you when Kennedy got shot?"

"Which Kennedy?" the hero replies wearily.

Paula shrugs. "Any Kennedy."

So where was Sharp when Bobby Kennedy was assassinated on June 4?

He'd left the Keys and was driving somewhere through the great American Southwest towards Los Angeles, the very scene of the assassination. There had been many diversions along the way. From Del Rio, Texas, across the enormity of that state into New Mexico, where Sharp came to the conclusion that American towns, sprawled around the nation's highways, "failed their landscape miserably." Across a dusty, wind-scraped plateau to the town of Hagerman, where he'd seen a picture of John F. Kennedy in a lonely filling station. In New Mexico the immensity of the landscape filled Sharp with fear. He drove on north of Albuquerque into the Nacimiento Mountains, adjacent to Navajo and Jicarilla Apache reservations. He pondered the historical fate of the Apaches as a once formidable but now utterly defeated people.

"For white men to be assassinating Negroes is a tacit admission of equality," he wrote. "No one is about to assassinate any Apaches in the near future; they are being left to inhabit a world from which the savor has been extracted." He moved on to Santa Fe, which "perhaps... quenched in me any remaining hope I might discover an individuality in American provincial towns."[42] He visited the New Mexican ghost town of Madrid, then crossed Arizona, Nevada, and California. Arriving in Los Angeles, he found it detestable, "In European terms, the ultimate non-city." Sharp wound up picnicking on Malibu Beach with "salami rolls, potato salad, and a bottle of plonque."[43] Then he got back into the car and escaped north into Big Sur.

Sharp's cross-country American road trip of 1968 – the pilgrimages to classic movie locales, the chance encounters and concurrent historical events – gave him a wealth of ideas and settings for screenplays. He came back the next year to do further exploring. He visited Colorado, Utah, and Montana, which included a visit to Little Big Horn. "Whether Custer's last stand was hubris or Nemesis is not clear," Sharp wrote. "Its vibrations are still to be felt however, coming up from a hundred years ago and his fate still exercises the imagination in ways that mightier destinies cannot."[44]

. . .

Arthur Penn had no such ambivalence about George Armstrong Custer. At the very time Sharp was at Little Big Horn, Penn was in advanced preparations to depict General Custer as a genocidal madman in *Little Big Man*.

In the aftermath of *Bonnie and Clyde*'s success, Hollywood executives could no longer deny Penn's instinct for the concerns of young audiences, although by now the director was forty-five years old. Actually, Penn was radicalising further. "Hollywood would probably prefer we didn't ask certain questions," Penn declared in the pivotal month of May 1968, "but I believe the point we have reached in film is no different from the crossroads that our entire culture has reached."[45]

Bonnie and Clyde was Penn's first contribution to the revolution in sensibilities. Now, with censorship in retreat, liberated heterosexual mischief went mainstream as an intentional affront to conservative America, the criminality of the Nixon administration, and the war-mongering establishment. The perpetrators included writers like Thomas McGuane, Philip Roth, Norman Mailer, and Leonard Michaels; actors Jack Nicholson, Dennis Hopper, Peter Fonda, and Elliot Gould; the cartoonist Robert Crumb; and the satirical musician Frank Zappa. Robert Altman's *M*A*S*H* and Bob Rafelson's *Five Easy Pieces*, both released in 1970, capture something of the spirit. The ghost of Lenny Bruce, who overdosed on morphine in 1966 while anticipating a prison sentence for obscenity, loomed over the orgy. If the style was sometimes crude and misogynist, it was dignified by its outrage at American hypocrisy.

In this climate, Penn was able to make two personal projects, irreverent and bawdy comedies that celebrated counter-cultural values. Penn's male heroes were distinct among his fellow agitators for their lack of aggressive machismo: Arlo Guthrie and Dustin Hoffman play innocent, gentle-hearted, diminutive American heroes pursued by carnal women. *Alice's Restaurant* (1969), inspired by Guthrie's song, is good-natured hokum about a hippie commune living in a converted church in Stockbridge, Massachusetts, and their short-lived dream of a new way of life. *Little Big Man* is a vastly more ambitious political western, culminating in a heretical retelling of Custer's Last Stand.

The allegorical possibilities of the western allowed filmmakers to indirectly address their outrage at the Vietnam War (only the flag-waving John Wayne was given the privilege of making a Vietnam War film while it still raged). Ralph Nelson's *Soldier Blue* (1970), for example, depicted a mass killing of Native Americans that was widely interpreted as an allusion to the 1968 My Lai massacre. But that was not the only reason Penn seized upon Thomas Berger's novel *Little Big Man* (1964), a picaresque reimagining of the historical genocide of Native Americans. Years later Penn said that he had been thinking "not so much [about] Vietnam, although, when it comes to wars of genocide, or genocidal attempts, they tend to resemble each other. I was really, in my mind, carrying the Holocaust."[46]

Penn was also determined to dismantle the western genre's sustaining myths of American history. He denounced how "American cinema has continually parodied and ridiculed Native Indians, depicting them as savage beasts, in order to justify the fact that we wiped them out. This might ease some people's conscience but I'm having none of it. I'm totally against this form of hypocrisy."[47] *Little Big Man* "starts out as a traditional genre piece," he explained, but then "you start asking yourself questions about the myths of the West and the way history has been falsified."[48]

. . .

Meanwhile, back in London and living in the exclusive area of Belsize Park[49], Sharp had started writing his own westerns.

The Greenock trilogy still remained to be completed. In late 1970 the UK publisher Michael Joseph announced publication of the final novel, *The Apple Pickers*, but that book never appeared.[50] Sharp's ambitions were drifting away from literary fiction. After penning a few more original scripts for British radio (*The Epitath*, broadcast in November 1968) and television (*A Sound from the Sea*, August 1970), he wrote near-exclusively for Hollywood

– a surprising career refocus after his unlikely success as an unashamedly literary novelist.

The shift to screenwriting would force Sharp to give up a measure of authorial control and become, in Jack Warner's classic phrase, just another schmuck with an Underwood. But after years of emotional chaos, he seemed relieved to abandon the egocentricity that came with being a romantic artist. He later reflected on his abandonment of the novel: "It's all bound up with the ego... are you this kind of writer, are you that kind of writer? I've been trying to dismantle defining myself by what kind of writer I am [...] I've gotten awfully sick of this whole Malcolm Lowry-Vincent Van Gogh 'let's talk to ourselves and write a masterpiece' sort of thing. I'd rather be happy and have my health than be a great writer."[51]

Sharp didn't make the change without reservations; he spoke of how screenwriting "makes you more imprecise with language" and "might atrophy your capacity to write."[52] But Sharp was off-target in his assessment of his strengths. Screenwriting steered him away from his worst tendencies. In his novels he had created characters through expansive interior monologues and wordy impressionistic sketches; now his characters had to come to life through tightly-plotted action and dialogue.

In any case, Sharp was ready to move away from the kind of autobiographical material he'd explored in the Greenock novels and in the plays for broadcast. "My fiction was about being Scottish and adolescent and provincial, and the plays sketches of the same landscape," he said.[53] The crime and western genres "satisfied some requirements of detachment from personal content and yet allowed me to write about themes that interested me."⁵⁴ It was not difficult for Sharp to write within the sensibilities of another culture, he said, "because the thing had already been formalised in me by all the movies I'd seen." In the western, for example, there was "a totally articulated landscape" that was "accessible to everybody."⁵⁵

But they change their sky, not their souls, who run across the sea. Sharp still wrote about lonely, emotionally wounded, not entirely sympathetic male characters. He again focused on the difficulties of relationships between men and women. But now his fatalistic pessimism would determine the trajectory of the narratives. Each of Sharp's first four produced screenplays concludes with the death of its hero by gunshot. Without discounting Sharp's original insights into America and its myths, his new screenplays were more than mere responses to this newly discovered country. The bleak vision was constitutional.

How did Sharp enter Hollywood so spectacularly? It happened in 1969 in London, where he established contacts in the industry. Impressing nearly everybody with his charm and intellect, he made fast friends. His writing seems to have resonated with adventurous young producers eager to explore the dark side of the era. Early that year he was hired to write a script called *No Tears* for the producer Julian Blaustein, a film that promised to focus on "the difficulty and importance of emotional honesty in relationships."⁵⁶ *No Tears* was never made, but around the same time Sharp sold options on three original screenplays to the producer Carter DeHaven III. This swag of scripts included two violent westerns about white and Native American relations

– *Billy Two Hats* and *Ulzana's Raid* – and a crime thriller set in Europe called *The Last Run*.

Shortly after Sharp made this deal, he made another with a former college professor named Mitchell Lifton. Lifton was attempting to enter the film industry by capitalising on Hollywood's upheaval. The studios were scrambling to adapt to the surprise success of youth-orientated pictures like Dennis Hopper's *Easy Rider* (1969). Lifton observed that "Hollywood executives are transformed. They are suddenly wearing roll neck sweaters, and chains, and growing their hair long."[57] Perhaps it could be a moment of opportunity for serious filmmakers? With that prospect, Lifton assumed responsibility for another of Sharp's westerns, *The Hired Hand*, and began to shop it around.

Set in the post-Civil War west, the quiet drama depicts the reconciliation of a drifter and his long-estranged wife and the consequent departure of the drifter's close male friend. Only the subplot grounds the film in the familiar generic territory of the western: a revenge drama that escalates in pointless eye-for-an-eye fashion to a shoot-out in the streets of a miserable town. Sharp said the bad guys were inspired by the lowlife mercenaries played by L.Q. Jones and Strother Martin in Sam Peckinpah's violent new western *The Wild Bunch*, which he had seen in London on original release that summer.[58]

Peter Fonda was sent the script when he was in London in October 1969 to promote *Easy Rider*. The enormous success of that film ensured its star the power to pick his next project. Fonda claimed to have read two hundred scripts in search of the right material. Although the original plan had been to shoot *The Hired Hand* in Italy, when Fonda read the screenplay he decided not only to accept the lead role but also to direct it as his first feature in America.[59] He cut a deal with Universal Studios to co-produce the movie with his company Pando Productions. In late May 1970 Fonda began filming on location in New Mexico with co-star Warren Oates.[60] Sharp and his family were on set until the writer departed for another road trip, this time in a studio Cadillac, down to Mexico to attend the FIFA World Cup.[61]

Meanwhile, Sharp's three earlier scripts moved forward. Carter DeHaven set up *The Last Run* with Metro-Goldwyn-Mayer. Sharp chose a classic chase plot for his first stab at the crime genre: a retired getaway driver named Harry Garmes, living in a Portuguese fishing village, agrees to come out of retirement to transport an escaped American convict from Spain to France. The convict's girlfriend tags along – a femme fatale who will seduce and betray Garmes. The operation goes to hell. Sharp described his script as "an attempt to use the melodramatic crime chase to deal with whatever the hero's preoccupations might be," in this case his loneliness, romantic yearnings, and grief since the death of his infant child.[62]

The film would be shot in locations around Andalucía. Several directors were attached to the project. British filmmaker John Boorman was an apt choice in light of his recent thriller *Point Blank* (1967), which had given a sometimes dreamlike, psychedelic quality to what was otherwise a taut thriller screenplay. But the filmmaker's rewrite of *The Last Run* (in collaboration with Bill Stair) was a radical departure from Sharp's original screenplay, and he soon left the project.[63]

So why not go directly to the master? Carter DeHaven next called on John Huston, for whom he'd recently produced two films in Europe. As one of the key contributors to the crime genre in cinema, Huston should have been ideal. He was a master of suspenseful dramas about untrusting cabals of criminals. Indeed, Sharp acknowledged that Harry Garmes was "almost straight out of Bogart, Hemingway, Huston." Lead actor George C. Scott compared Garmes to the Bogart of *Key Largo*, "an adventurous semi-hero, a lonely man who suddenly commits himself to an impossible undertaking and, usually, winds up face down full of bullet holes."[64] And yet *The Last Run* was not an uncritical homage.

Harry Garmes was clearly an exhausted incarnation of that heroic archetype; the story tells of his alienation and the ultimate futility of his return to crime. His fatal error is believing in the possibility of love. Unlike Bogart's hero, Garmes dies of his bullet wounds. It is tempting to read an element of patricide into Sharp's dismantling of the Bogart hero, but that was no automatic reason to discount Huston's suitability as director.

Sharp described Garmes as:

> *... a man with a limited comprehension of existence. He's not interested, shall we say, in Beethoven, tennis, certain kinds of food or social discourse: he's not particularly interested in politics. He is interested in filtering his ill-defined, but strong emotions to the surface and allowing the sun to warm them... He is attempting to re-enter life. He fails because he is too limited a man, but he makes drama of the attempt because he is a strong man... He's a first-stage prototype, I suppose*

– a kind of clearing of the undergrowth in terms of trying to write the romantic hero.[65]

By January 1971 filming was underway. Sharp was installed at Granada's Alhambra Palace Hotel and extensively rewrote the script to accommodate Huston's ideas. Writing for a director who had profoundly influenced Sharp's early imaginative life must have initially seemed like a dream come true – after all, Huston's *African Queen* had given Sharp a fantasy vision of his long lost parents – but the collaboration was a disaster. Huston himself rewrote parts of the script with his twenty-year-old son, Tony, and insisted on interpolating a new scene set in the Plaza de Toros in Mijas: the escaped convict would impulsively enter the bullring and bring the bull in for several passes with the cape. When actor Tony Mussante was too intimidated to perform the stunt with live bulls, Huston characteristically jumped in to demonstrate. The scene had to be written out again, although was later revived for Huston's 1984 film of Malcolm Lowry's *Under the Volcano*.

Sharp was finally disillusioned with the director. In later years he described Huston as "a real sadist."[66] On location, he told a reporter:

I'm not one of these guys who feels, 'It's my masterpiece, nobody must touch it.'... What gets me is when they come to me and say: 'I don't know quite what it is I want, but that isn't it. Give me something else.' And then when I give it to them, I see the director, the director's assistant, even the director's 20-year-old boy play around with it until they've got it all screwed up – no characterization, no motivation, no nothing – and then they come back to me again and they tell me that won't work, we can't use this, try giving us something else. That makes it pretty damned hard to function.[67]

George C. Scott was also unhappy with Huston's departures from Sharp's original story. The fight between star and director made international news. After a few weeks Huston departed and, in typically irrepressible style, almost immediately directed another masterpiece, *Fat City* (1972). Richard Fleischer was called in to direct *The Last Run*. Fleischer hated the current draft of the script; he believed Huston had eliminated the best parts of Sharp's first draft. So Sharp dutifully put together a seventh and final draft that satisfied the new regime.[68]

Despite the production troubles, *The Last Run* turned out to be an excellent neo-noir. Centering on American characters but projecting a European sensibility, it fits into the crime genre alongside unsentimental contemporary stories of the French gangster milieu, themselves inspired by American hardboiled prototypes – the *romans noirs* of Jean-Patrick Manchette, the *romans durs* of Georges Simenon, and the films of Jean-Pierre Melville and Jacques Deray.

Sharp's films began to appear in American cinemas in the summer of 1971 – *The Last Run* in early July, *The Hired Hand* a month later. Although neither film was a box office hit, their failures did not yet derail Alan Sharp's rising career in the movies. The Sharps moved to Los Angeles. It made sense to be based in Hollywood, and it also gave Sharp an opportunity to escape what he described as "that whole Femalestrom [*sic*.] I was in."[69]

. . .

Arthur Penn's period of righteous rage, irreverent humour, and progressive hopes waned as America entered the 1970s. After the exhausting scale of the production of *Little Big Man* in Calgary and Montana – his fifth film in six years – Penn was a burnt-out case. He found himself in an identity crisis. He later explained, "The reasons I got depressed are very personal, it's pretty complicated." He said he hoped "to be able to make a film about it one day."[70] He took a break from his career, deciding that "it was a period when it seemed more important to spend time with my wife and children."[71]

Penn's son Matthew remembers: "He really had been away from the family for quite a number of years. He was coming off three very different but rather extraordinary successes. My sister and I had gotten older, and I know he made a conscious choice to try to be home with the family, and a participant in our lives in a way he was not able to be during the shooting of those pictures."[72]

In 1972 Penn agreed to make a short segment for an ensemble documentary film, *Visions of Eight*, about the Munich Olympics in September. The event, however, was devastated by the deaths of eleven Israeli athletes in a siege by Palestinian terrorists. At the commencement of the crisis Matthew and Molly were at the airport, about to fly back to New York. Penn and his wife Peggy were caught up in Munich's chaos until they were able to escape to Italy.

"They were both, along with the rest of the world, in a real depression about what had happened," Matthew Penn recalls.

Munich was yet another violent political trauma touching directly on Penn's life. He had had a personal connection to both assassinated Kennedy brothers. Penn had advised John F. Kennedy in his TV debate with Richard Nixon in 1960.[73] President Kennedy's assassination in 1963, Penn said, was "as if the country had suffered a heart attack. After that nothing would be the same again."[74] The nightmare did not end. Penn had met Robert Kennedy to discuss campaign commercials shortly before the senator's fatal trip to California in 1968.[75]

Matthew Penn recalls, "In the case of both assassinations, Dad was just devastated. I remember a number of occasions when he was really quite tearful, certainly the morning after Robert Kennedy was shot. He told me he was deeply upset for the Kennedy family but also for the country. Nobody knew in exactly which direction we were going to turn. And I think he felt in the case of both Kennedys there was a hope there that was never fulfilled."

Although Penn was aware of the brothers' limitations, he recognised their symbolic worth for the progressive movement. "John wasn't the kind of hero we turned him into, even if he did personify the hopes of all those who had ideals back then, to the extent that we projected those hopes onto him. With his death, and then Bobby's, a part of our existence and aspirations came to an end."[76]

Penn began to ruminate on "an atmosphere of psychosis at a certain point that seems to take over in [a] society that permits assassination – not only permits it but invites it." After the death of the Kennedys, Penn later recalled, "I was in shock, quite frankly, and I just had to do a film about it."[77]

. . .

In *Little Big Man* Penn had idealised Native Americans as "human beings" in opposition to genocidal whites. Sharp, by contrast, approached the historical subject of the Indian Wars with bitter pessimism. In early 1972 director Robert Aldrich filmed Sharp's western *Ulzana's Raid* in Arizona and Nevada. With a conventional scenario of a U.S. Cavalry hunt for a marauding band of Apaches, *Ulzana's Raid* was in the tradition of John Ford's *Fort Apache* (1948), Sam Peckinpah's *Major Dundee* (1965), and also a previous Aldrich picture, *Apache* (1954), starring Burt Lancaster as an escaped warrior. Now Lancaster took the starring role of McIntosh, a world-weary Indian scout, resigned to the unbridgeable differences in the worldviews of the whites and the Apaches. Hating an Apache, McIntosh says, "would be like hating the desert because there ain't no water in it."

On *Ulzana*, Sharp found himself caught between the visions of two strong-willed creative artists. Aldrich and Lancaster, prominent Hollywood liberals, saw the potential for the film to say something about the Vietnam War, although neither included Sharp in that discussion.[78] Sharp was less interested in contemporary political allegories, anyway; he preferred to explore the ways the harsh landscape of Arizona had shaped what he thought of as the "innate Apache capacity for torture." In 1968 Sharp had observed first-hand the American Southwest and concluded it was "a country which could only breed in its original beholders a stony malevolence, a cruelty that was as unremitting as it was functional."[79]

While Sharp was no overt western revisionist like Penn, motivated by political antagonism to the genre itself, neither

George C. Scott as Harry Garmes in *The Last Run*;
Jack Warden as Sheriff Gifford in *Billy Two Hats*

would he uncritically perpetuate its timeworn triumphant myths. Brutally pessimistic on the compatibility of white and Native American worldviews, *Ulzana's Raid* attempted a far more intellectually serious grappling with history than *Little Big Man*. Sharp's screenplay was the basis for a deeply unsettling film containing possibly the bloodiest depiction of Native American atrocities against civilian whites in the history of Hollywood.

Strangely, for what Lancaster and Aldrich supposedly intended to be a left-wing Vietnam War allegory, the drama does not conclude with a massacre of innocent Apaches by the cavalry – the bleak denouement, the My Lai, which seems inevitable for much of the film. Such a massacre would have counterbalanced the numerous Apache horrors in the earlier part of the film, putting the "civilized" whites and "savage" Apaches in abysmal moral equivalence, each side equally capable of atrocities in this war as in Vietnam. *Ulzana's Raid* is about as far from Penn's hippie idealism as can be imagined.

Ulzana's Raid was released by United Artists in December 1972, shortly after Richard Nixon won his second term in a landslide. Aldrich's direction in the sun-bleached desert is without a shred of glamour. Lancaster's performance was one of his best in a repertoire of wildly variable quality, and he would become a long-term supporter of Alan Sharp.

Meanwhile Sharp had flown back to London to revise his earlier screenplay *Billy Two Hats* for director Ted Kotcheff, a globe-trotting journeyman. It became the first western shot in Israel. Production began in late 1972, with Gregory Peck as an unlikely Scotsman, in the nervous weeks after the Munich terrorist attack.[80] The film's release would be delayed until 1974.

Like *The Last Run*, *Billy Two Hats* is a chase story. A good-natured Scottish bank robber and his younger friend Billy Two Hats, a youth with part-Native American ancestry, flee from the law. The vengeance-obsessed Sheriff Gifford is a racist and a bigot. The world he thought he knew is crumbling. He responds to what he doesn't understand, such as the genuine love between Billy and a much-abused mail-order bride, with brutal violence. But he also proves capable of generosity and good-humour. He resembles Harry Garmes, another figure of middle-aged isolation and confusion – the intellectually limited macho in crisis. In his screenplays, Sharp made a point of interrogating the limits of generic masculine archetypes.

As things stood in the early 1970s there was little in the work of Sharp and Penn to suggest compatibility for a future collaboration. But at that time Penn began "looking for a film to deal with… the loss of confidence and optimism that I associate with the American temperament."[81] For a while the future of America looked as bleak as the final pages of an Alan Sharp screenplay.

2. An End of Wishing
(1972-1973)

Now based in Hollywood, Alan Sharp wrote another original screenplay called *Tepic in the Morning*. Sharp registered a 144-page draft with the Library of Congress for US copyright purposes in early February 1972[82], and made plans to direct the film himself in Mexico that summer.

The story was another Bogart-Huston pastiche enriched by his experience. The idea had come to Sharp while passing through the city of Tepic on his Mexican road trip in 1970. He'd had the uncanny experience of stepping out of reality and into a familiar movie landscape. Early one morning, he told readers of the *Los Angeles Times*, he'd sat in the bar of the Tepic train station and found himself in "the setting for a Bogart movie, the seedy expatriate, enduring his existence, drinking cognac with his morning coffee."

Of course, Alan Sharp was hardly as broke as Fred C. Dobbs in *The Treasure of the Sierra Madre* (1948), but he let his imagination play and threw in a dash of the novel *To Have and Have Not* (1937): "You know how it is in Tepic in the mornings," he wrote, the voice of the classic

Hemingway insider taking us into his confidence. Outside "in the square in front of the church there were people awake and busy, coming from market, having their shoes polished, reading the paper." A fat man in the bar put raw eggs in his orange juice. "He was doubtless a character in the movie," Sharp decided. "When the 7.15 train came in the young Rita Hayworth would get off, come to find her embezzler husband or coward brother. Between her and Bogart would pass a glance, half knowing, part guessing: a recognition from which the plot would unwind."[83]

Sharp went back to America and wrote something in that general spirit. But the script would depart from convention. In 1971 he described a scenario

> ... in which we set up the thriller framework, then don't use it. [We have] the standard thriller scene – the expatriate in the small Mexican town, the arrival of the girl, the corrupt police official, the stolen money... then we leave the framework [...] [It's] like being in a huge expensive house with all these rooms and bathrooms and beds and you put a sleeping bag down on the floor. I hope it's a kind of alienation effect.[84]

But the planned 1972 production did not go ahead, and *Tepic* was put on hold (it was finally realised as *Little Treasure* in 1985, the only film Sharp would direct himself).[85] The screenplay centres on a character directly inspired by Paula of the Florida Keys.[86] Margo is a former stripper who comes down to an unnamed town in Mexico – Sharp ultimately filmed in Tepoztlán and other locations in the states of Morelos and Durango[87] – at the invitation of her long-absent father, a former bank robber. While there she meets an American expatriate, Eugene – "to a marked extent a

Harry Garmes, but I hope he's one stage further on," Sharp said of his original conception[88] – who is drifting through the remote towns of Mexico projecting movies.

After her father dies, Margo drags Eugene back to America on a Quixotic search for her dad's long-buried and possibly mythical loot in the ghost towns of New Mexico. To fund the search Margo returns to topless dancing in a nightclub. Eugene works behind the bar. The film does for a time leave its framework – in a vague and meandering way. As a stripper, Margot refuses to 'drop her string' and appear bottomless. When she transgresses this personal rule at the insistence of a wealthy client at a private party, she has an emotional breakdown. The relationship goes to hell: the obsessive Margo shoots Eugene when he decides to call off the search for the loot. For a change, however, the hero's gunshot wound is not fatal. Although it was by far the weakest of his initial fistful of screenplays, Sharp would stick with the project for years.

But the collapse of the 1972 production did not stop Sharp's career momentum. He was established in Hollywood and had come a long way from Greenock. Living with his family in a house with a pool in the vicinity of the legendary Chateau Marmont, Sharp developed a fondness for water volleyball.[89] The dismally-received film *Myra Breckinridge* (1970) had been shot at the Marmont, and Dan Sharp remembers that his father tried in vain to persuade 20th Century Fox to give him the film's large statue of Gore Vidal's transgender heroine "so he could put it in our yard next to where it had stood in the movie."[90]

"It was full-on hippie time in LA," remembers Liz Sharp. Although their home was not drug-orientated, it "was always full of people who would come and forget to leave. We had two film students from London. One of them stayed for three months, one stayed a year. Despite a lot of it being harrowing, Alan had enormous energy. We had a lot of good fun."

With *Tepic in the Morning* on hold, Sharp began writing a new spec screenplay, a private detective story, reusing some of the same basic elements – the Paula archetype, Mexican treasure, a thriller framework to be abandoned mid-drama – as well other gleanings from his visits to Key West and Los Angeles in 1968. The working title was for a time *An End of Wishing*, and throughout its production it was *The Dark Tower*, a reference to Browning's 'Childe Rolande to the Dark Tower Came' (1855, its title drawn from a speech in *King Lear*). Roland is an apprentice knight, and the dark tower is generally considered to be the object of his quest, although what it contains remains a mystery.[91] The title would not be changed to *Night Moves* until post-production.

Based on the quality of Sharp's work-in-progress, producer Robert M. Sherman arranged to help fund the writing process. Sherman had formerly been at the CMA talent agency and then became a production executive at 20th Century Fox.[92] Now he worked with directors Mark Rydell and Sydney Pollack as president of Sanford Productions, founded in 1971. With Warner Bros., Sanford had produced Rydell's *The Cowboys* (1972) and Pollack's *Jeremiah Johnson* (1972). Their latest production was Jerry Schatzberg's road movie *Scarecrow* (1973) starring Gene Hackman and Al Pacino.[93] Sherman remembered Sharp asking at the outset, "Should I make this a typical detective story about a guy trying to solve a crime or should I make this what I really would like it to be, which is about a guy trying to solve *himself*?" Sherman urged Sharp to take the later approach.[94] He proved to be an enlightened, passionate producer who would see the project through to completion.

Sharp made his usual good impression on his new associates. Bonnie Bruckheimer, Sherman's assistant, remembers that "Alan was one of the most entertaining, fascinating, and interesting men I had ever met. He was funny beyond belief, charming, and knocked the socks off everyone who met him."[95]

Sharp began writing his unconventional detective movie during the Watergate scandal, a period of ever-worsening political malaise in the United States. He recognised a mood of disillusionment after the hopeful sixties. Unsurprisingly, Sharp's writerly response was to explore the American darkness through the most hopelessly fatalistic strain of the film noir tradition. The sensibility is best indicated by Sharp's near-quotation of a piece of dialogue written by Daniel Mainwaring for the classic *Out of the Past* (1947). In Sharp's screenplay, the detective's wife will ask which team is winning a football game. "Nobody," answers the detective. "One side's losing slower than the other."[96] Sharp was not alone in pursuing this strain among filmmakers of the period, although commercial successes in the bleakly confrontational mode were rare.

In fact, American audiences were turning away from the present to the comforts of an imagined past. Perhaps nostalgia allowed audiences to transcend the profound ideological divisions entrenched by the 1960s. In any case, Hollywood discovered that America as it had ostensibly existed in earlier decades was a highly commercializable cinematic landscape. Peter Bogdanovich's *The Last Picture Show* (1971) was among the earliest of the new wave of successful period films, and other constitutionally upbeat New Hollywood directors found success with well-crafted, essentially optimistic historical evocations. 1973 was the watershed year. That year's biggest US box office hits included George Lucas's *American Graffiti* (set in 1962), George Roy Hill's heist flick *The Sting* (the 1930s), and Pollack's *The Way We Were* (the 1930s-1950s).

Meanwhile, broadcast television continued to revive what had been the cultural ephemera of earlier decades – old movies. What would soon be called Hollywood's golden age became one of the touchstones of a fractured culture. Among their other attractions, old movies had camp value. They represented a sensibility that had shifted. By now several not-long-dead Hollywood stars had already acquired iconic status, most notably James Dean (dead 1955), Humphrey Bogart (1957), and Marilyn Monroe (1962).

A cult-like fandom had formed around Bogart in the decade after his death, often said to have originated in yearly film screenings at the Brattle cinema at Harvard.[97] Bogartmania quickly went mainstream. Stephen Frears' *Gumshoe* (1971) spoofed the Bogart detective film, and Woody Allen's 1969 Broadway hit *Play It Again, Sam* (adapted for cinema in 1972) used a trench-coated Bogart as its protagonist's imaginary friend and romantic advisor.

The posthumous elevation of Bogart to icon coincided with the nostalgic revival of the hardboiled detective story he had dominated in the movies. Bogart had played the genre's two greatest detectives: Dashiell Hammett's

Sam Spade (in Huston's *The Maltese Falcon*, 1941) and Raymond Chandler's Philip Marlowe (in Howard Hawks' *The Big Sleep*, 1946). Hollywood sought a workable commercial formula to capitalise on this interest, and at first they returned to the original source material. Chandler's novel *The Little Sister* (1944) became *Marlowe* (Paul Bogart, 1969) starring James Garner and adapted to contemporary Los Angeles. Paul Magwood directed a semi-tribute called *Chandler* (1971), starring Warren Oates as a private detective of that name.

These initial attempts to revive the genre were stale. Leigh Brackett, co-screenwriter of *The Big Sleep*, wrote in 1974:

Everything that was fresh and exciting about Philip Marlowe in the forties had become a cliché, outworn by imitation and overuse [...] Time had removed the context. The Los Angeles upon which Chandler based his literary work is as dead as Babylon. [...] We don't speak that language any more. We've got a whole new generation and a whole new bag of clichés – just as phony but different.[98]

Sharp's *Dark Tower* screenplay, with its characters' jokes about old Bogart movies (as well as Sharp's subtler Bogart references[99]), indicates the campiness of the private detective genre by the early 1970s. It shares this generic self-awareness with the two other great revisionist detective films that beat it to the screen. *The Long Goodbye*, co-written by Brackett, features an incidental character who imitates old movie star voices. *Chinatown*, actually set in the 1930s, begins with a joke about the detective's inevitable venetian blinds – "I just had them installed on Wednesday," he says. But while both of these films start off as mere pastiche, they each pull the same trick of shifting midway into serious examinations of corruption and betrayal.

In *The Dark Tower* Sharp pokes fun at the status of the private detective by the 1970s, an easily ridiculed movie cliché. Detective Harry Moseby is slightly embarrassed by the name of his firm, Moseby Confidential, although, he jokes, at least there isn't an eye printed on his business card. His client teasingly asks if he is incorruptible in the Philip Marlowe tradition, if neither "bribes, beatings" nor "the allure of a woman's body" will get him to abandon a case.[100] But this riffing functions as more than a wink at a movie-literate audience. Sharp cleverly uses the very corniness of the loner private eye to emphasise Harry's general obsolescence – an old-fashioned individualist resisting the modern age. His friendly rival Nick, who runs a computerised agency, occasionally sends a case Harry's way when he "needs a real live detective and not one of our machines."[101]

Sharp brought his own interpretation to his chosen film genres. He said:

The western and the detective story represent to me the two most interesting film forms. One was 'Before the Fall' – man, if you like, before psycho-analysis, before he became self-conscious when reacting to the landscape, when the elements were hostile and he reacted in a certain way. He didn't have to introspect. He was primitive man in a form, and that interested me. The detective story, on the other hand, represents 'after the Fall', when man started having to solve things, and what he basically had to solve was his own life. That's what the detective – allegorically – is doing, trying to find the meaning of life.[102]

Sharp actually brought to the detective story a modicum of real-world experience. He had worked as a private investigator's assistant as a teenager in Scotland. His first assignment was to meet a stranger on a train to collect a mysterious object, which was ultimately revealed to be a gas cooker.[103] Sharp quickly realised he had been apprenticed to "a sherry alcoholic who was basically a debt-collector."[104] The job didn't last long. Harry Moseby's work at the outset of the screenplay, a bargain basement shamus mediating petty suburban squabbles, is hardly any more glamorous than that.

. . .

In his early drafts, Sharp recalled, he set up a conventional investigation scenario.[105] As the set-up survives in the film, Harry Moseby is hired to find Delly Grastner, a runaway promiscuous sixteen-year-old. The investigation coincides with troubles in Harry's marriage to Ellen, an antiques dealer. By chance he discovers Ellen's infidelity and quickly traces and confronts the other man. Harry leaves this tumultuous, unresolved situation in Los Angeles to seek Delly in New Mexico and then in the Florida Keys, where he finds the girl living in a strange, vaguely incestuous romantic triangle with her former stepfather, Tom Iverson, and his present girlfriend, Paula. While diving at night Delly discovers a drowned pilot in a crashed plane. Harry has a brief fling with Paula before he returns Delly to her mother in Los Angeles. Then Delly is killed in a supposed accident which appears to be sabotage.

Using the same gimmick as *Tepic in the Morning*, Sharp had originally planned to jettison the generic framework at some point, to "take the crime and the story so far and then discard it," shifting focus to the blooming relationship of Harry and Paula. There would be no revelation of the culprit. "I wanted to avoid who it was going to be, by not having it be anybody,"[106] Sharp remembered. His signature fatalism would appear again in full force: "I initially wanted Moseby and Paula to take off on a trip, ostensibly with the boodle, so there would be some basic narrative. I meant it to be a love relationship trip that would end in disaster as well."[107] But nevertheless "the brutal aspect of the piece, the 'who did what to whom' thing, was intended to just stream behind as a correlation, but not be what the piece was all about."[108]

In the early stages of the screenplay's development at Sanford Productions, Sydney Pollack and Mark Rydell read the work-in-progress and passed along their suggestions.[109] But then the Sanford partnership was dissolved. Sherman started a new company, Layton Productions, named after the street where he lived in Brentwood, Los Angeles.[110] He was now solely responsible for *The Dark Tower*. He sent copies of an unfinished draft around Hollywood. According to Sherman, Warner Brothers' studio chief John Calley made the strongest offer by promising to sign a major director. Calley told Sherman, "I can get you Bogdanovich, Penn, or Kubrick. Can anybody at Fox do that?"[111]

The *Los Angeles Times* announced the Warner Brothers deal with Layton Productions for *The Dark Tower* on March 31, 1973. Nevertheless, the screenplay was not finished and Sharp was losing confidence in his ability to write a conclusion for his unresolved whodunit. More crucially, Warner Brothers was uneasy with his plan to abandon the genre framework mid-drama. The studio sought that major director who would help Sharp finish the script. John Frankenheimer was considered, and then Arthur Penn. "I really didn't think the script was good enough to send to Penn, and I protested," remembered Sharp.[112]

. . .

After his long hiatus from feature filmmaking, Arthur Penn chose to come back to direct the work of two writers, Alan Sharp and Thomas McGuane, in successive projects produced by Robert Sherman. Although as writers they pursued different obsessions, Sharp and McGuane had a lot in common. They were both acclaimed literary novelists who had turned to writing westerns for the screen. Their screenplays would attract a number of actors from the same talent pool, including Warren Oates, Peter Fonda and Margot Kidder. Both were charismatic, athletic, and wild-living. McGuane, after surviving a motorcycle crash in the early seventies, had decided to abandon caution and indulge his tendency to excess; his nickname was Captain Berserko. Less happily, both writers would prove to be lacklustre directors of their own screenplays. As a filmmaker, Penn had seemingly little in common with the sensibilities of either writer but perhaps he was curious about what might emerge from potentially combative collaborations. Perhaps he simply didn't know how to proceed in his career.

Penn signed on to direct *The Dark Tower* in the spring of 1973.[113] Work on the screenplay was delayed by a Writers' Guild of America strike that lasted from March 6 to June 24. This left a mere three months to get it done before the commencement of filming, concurrent with the many responsibilities of pre-production. Associate Producer Gene Lasko assisted this process. Matthew Penn remembers that although Lasko's main contribution to Penn's films was in casting, he also served as "a sounding board. He and Dad would discuss story." Lasko contributed some ideas and lines of dialogue, and he and Penn discussed the project at length without Sharp's participation. "It wasn't even a question of being excluded," Sharp remembered. "I don't think we did the right thing in the writing process. I don't think we got it right, and we all have our responsibilities there."[114]

Sharp became frustrated with what he saw as Penn's indecision about the character at this stage of the process. "I expected Arthur at some time to step in and say 'O.K. here's my hero; this is my Moseby,' which I felt was not only his right, but his duty as an *auteur* director. That never really came out."[115] For his part, Penn remembered: "The general spirit of the script remained the same but [...] I made a great number of modifications and additions in collaboration with Sharp. The film is very different from his original script."[116] Penn took credit for making Harry more jealous, aggressive, and unlikeable – characteristics which would hinder the detective's ability to solve the case.[117]

The generic archetypes in *The Dark Tower* screenplay – the detective, the missing girl, the femme fatale – were written to upset expectations. Despite Sharp's evident fondness for the genre, he was determined to disassemble the classic figure of the knightly private detective as Chandler had defined him: "Down these mean streets a man must go who is not himself mean, who is neither tarnished nor afraid."[118] Penn seems to have had hardly any affection for the classic detective hero at all. He said, "I like Bonnie and Clyde a lot better than I like Harry Moseby. Anyone who does stuff like detective work and spy work and CIA work – they're just the dregs of the barrel as far as I'm concerned."[119]

Harry Moseby's shortcomings help shape the dramatic arc of the film. Harry has antecedents in earlier Alan Sharp characters, and shares his surname with one of the main figures in the Greenock novels. He suffers the lonely yearnings of Harry Garmes in *The Last Run* and some of the macho bigotry of Sherriff Gifford in *Billy Two Hats*. Like those earlier characters, Harry confronts a world he can no longer comprehend. He hangs on in desperation to his professional routine. Like Garmes and Gifford, Harry's capacity for sudden physical brutality sits uneasily with his introspective tendencies. Sharp compared Harry to Macbeth, "the guy who, in the end, is only free when acting, but whose life is mostly strangled by thought. Moseby was that, but on a much lower point on the scale."[120]

While Harry may act the thuggish philistine with others, on his own he plays chess, a hobby Sharp included to "represent Harry as an introspective, internalised man of action."[121] Harry replays a 1922 match between K. Emmrich and Bruno Moritz at Bad Oyenhaussen in Hamburg. Moritz missed the opportunity to win by "three little knight moves... He didn't see it."[122] Moritz's supposed obliviousness to the obvious serves as a useful metaphor for Harry's predicament as an investigator. Here Sharp was engaging with Raymond Chandler's symbolic repertoire. In *The Big Sleep*, when Marlowe discovers the nymphomaniac Carmen Sternwood naked in his bed – and does not accept her invitation – he reconsiders his last move on the chessboard. "The move with the knight was wrong. I put it back where I had moved it from. Knights had no meaning in this game.

It wasn't a game for knights."[123] The chivalric hero is redundant in this world of corruption; Marlowe, who observes the knightly code, is a man out of time.

The shooting script – and, even more explicitly, Alan Sharp's subsequent novelization, told through Harry's claustrophobic point-of-view – unambiguously depict the detective in the midst of a profound identity crisis at the outset of the drama. The novelization emphasises Harry's urban alienation. He sees in the sprawl of Los Angeles "a landscape that undermined his basic belief that there was a solution to everything, that missing girls could be found."[124] He privately recognises that his old certainties are crumbling: "Like a lot of other things, politics and ecology and war, he wasn't certain what he felt or thought or knew."[125] While ruminating on Zuma Beach "he felt old, far back fears turn in him, fears of being out of the circle of love, of warmth, of light. His sense of what he was, the story he told himself each day to make sense of his doings, seemed a contrived and paltry narrative."[126]

At the same time, Harry is scared of going beyond the existing limits of his understanding, to question his core beliefs. Meeting his wife's lover Marty Heller, Harry knows that "there resided in him nuances and doubts that he, Moseby, would never achieve. To live, however, in that other world, the mind ceaselessly questioning, questing, undermining its own foundations in a search for some final bottom – that was an even bleaker prospect."[127]

The novelization elaborates the backstory of Harry's marriage. Ellen had married him in the belief that this one-time professional football player had buried depths and sensitivities; as Harry characterises it, because he was "not as dumb as he looks." But he had failed to open up his "central self-containment"[128] to her. Ellen is the primary breadwinner and disapproves of his sleazy profession as a detective. Feeling unfairly judged and emasculated, Harry had become "more jaundiced" in his view of *her* profession and contemptuous of her social circle – variously gay, cosmopolitan, intellectual, from "the world of films and television."[129] At the commencement of the drama, as the certainties in his life continue to evaporate, Harry has doubled down on his self-styled redneck, philistine persona as a mask for his insecurities and as a response to these tensions within his marriage.

Harry's conventional macho thinking will lead him to frequently misjudge the other characters. He is attracted to the simple machismo of Hollywood stuntmen and finds companionship with Joey Ziegler, who flatters Harry's ego by remembering his moment of glory with the Oakland Raiders at the 1963 Pro Bowl. They reminisce fondly of the brainless certainties of Harry's football-playing days. Later Harry considers leaving the detective business to perform stuntman work with Zeigler.[130]

To Sharp, stunt men had:

... the outward appurtenances of the American male hero and there's a touch of country and western singers about them. They're perfectly good about risking life and limb and of being terse and jocund about it, but they're as boring as shit. These three [Zeigler, Marv Ellman, and Tom Iverson] were intended to represent the football team from which Moseby had come, with the simplicity of their perception of life.[131]

Sharp later reflected: "Moseby's life has always been lived in a frame of reference which says, 'if you ask the right questions you get the right answers.' The whole film is an attempt to disprove that to Moseby's dissatisfaction." He added, "In various ways, I rated all of the women much more highly than anybody else in the movie."[132] Part of the screenplay's enduring appeal is its autonomous female characters who slip away from the usual functions demanded by generic convention.

Sharp's investigative plot updates a genre stalwart, the "wandering daughter job," as Hammett described it in his 1929 *Black Mask* story "Fly Paper." A sexually promiscuous girl or young woman has rebelled against her wealthy background. She has developed, in Hammett's words, "a kink that made her dislike the polished side of life, like the rough."[133] Hired by her family, the detective typically encounters a chain of murders instigated in some part by the girl's unchecked hunger for sexual adventure. A classic incarnation is Chandler's twenty-year-old Carmen Sternwood. After reconsidering his move on the chessboard, Marlowe is so disgusted with Carmen's animal-like sexuality and repeated attempts to seduce him that he throws her out of his apartment. He narrates: "I went back to the bed and looked down at it. The imprint of her head was still in the pillow, of her small corrupt body still on the sheets. I put my empty glass down and tore the bed to pieces savagely."[134] Carmen is a killer, and by the story's end she is put into an institution.

But by the 1970s female promiscuity did not have to be so bluntly condemned as an expression of the death drive. The sexually liberated young drifter had become a new

Hollywood archetype – just as phony but different – and part of the industry's generally feeble attempts to imagine the hippie subculture on screen. The object of jokes about personal hygiene, she was nevertheless desirable, carefree, and promiscuous without hang-ups. Two examples appeared in films released in 1973. Clint Eastwood's *Breezy* and John G. Avildsen's *Save The Tiger* both featured sweet-hearted young hippies (Kay Lenz and Laurie Heineman, respectively) who doggedly seduce haggard, fifty-something, and initially reluctant businessmen (William Holden and Jack Lemmon). Both movies flattered the prejudices of men on the wrong side of the generation gap.

Alan Sharp was not interested in perpetuating such lazy male fantasies. His wandering daughter, Delly, is a sympathetic and believable character. Sharp's oldest daughter was about Delly's age at the time he wrote the script, and he was aware of the challenges of cross-generational communication. In his experience,

> *... people much younger than you only seemingly share the same language. You have a verbal commonality but no content commonality. You don't know anything the other person means and Delly was living proof that, in a way, there is no communication to be had... Delly was somebody whose fusion with life was both enchanting and totally inaccessible. She represents, I suppose, the kind of amoral innocence which you can have no conception of, until you are way beyond being able to engage in it. In the film, she's there to prod Moseby with a sense of how encased he is with his thoughts about things.*[135]

While most characters in *The Dark Tower* simply mock Delly's precocious sex life – "When we all get liberated like Delly, there's going to be fighting in the streets" and "Delly's idea of a commune was her and the guy on top of her."[136] – Sharp makes clear that Delly's promiscuity is not generic nymphomania. She is seeking attention and rebelling against her parasitic mother, the former B-movie actress Arlene Iverson. Harry suggests to Arlene that Delly is "trying to even the score."[137] Indeed all of Delly's known conquests are either her mother's ex-lovers, or in the case of Quentin, the type of young man her mother considers a "freak" and a "creep."[138] Arlene is jealous rather than concerned for a vulnerable teenager involved with much older men (including Arlene's former husband).

Harry, in the knightly Marlowe tradition, does not succumb to Delly's repeated advances, which soon become something of a running joke between them. But Delly is no Carmen Sternwood. Harry realises that Delly is an unhappy and exploited teenager in need of protection.

For his femme fatale, Sharp again drew inspiration from the woman he'd met five years earlier in the Florida Keys. This time he gave the character the same first name. His fictional Paula Hirsch is sardonic and verbally playful. Harry will eventually tire of Paula's "ping pong talk"[139] but initially, at least, he finds her fascinating. She quotes or misquotes *Othello*, Robert Browning, and Robert Louis Stevenson. The references puzzle Harry some of the time, as the novelization will make clear. The beast with two backs? Home is the hunter? Harry feels like he is "sailing" on "oceans of incomprehension."[140]

Paula is without illusions and ambitions. As a femme fatale, her criminal complicity will give her little beyond "some change, a little more fuel for the flight, a bus ticket to the next stop after Key West."[141] When prompted, Paula recalls her past bluntly – "I taught school, I kept house, I waited tables, I did a little stripping and I did a little hooking, and I trod a lot of water."[142] Sharp acknowledged the "tarnished angel aspect" of Paula's generic role but dismissed a personal history of "stripping and shagging" as "male clichés of degradation." He recalled that Harry Garmes in *The Last Run* had refused to condemn the prostitute Monique. Garmes quotes to her a poetic line Sharp apparently invented: "'She's not a whore who sleeps abed with thee, and he, and me. She's a whore who has the heart of a whore.' Believe me, I know."[143]

Paula is Sharp's second attempt to reinvent the femme fatale in the crime genre. Like Claudie in *The Last Run*, Paula seduces the hero at the behest of a criminal lover in order to manipulate him. Yet while fulfilling their generic function, neither Paula nor Claudie are standard-issue remorseless evil-doers. On the contrary, they are largely sympathetic. Paula's manipulative seduction of Harry is completely unconventional and not very seductive at all. In fact, Harry winds up pleasuring her. She manages to be simultaneously deceptive while genuinely reaching for, as the script puts it, "some solace, some comfort" after the upsetting discovery of the drowned pilot's body in the waters of the Keys.[144]

. . .

During the months of writing with Penn, Sharp agreed to abandon his original plan to allow the mystery to dissipate and remain unsolved. Now Sharp had to tie up the open-ended narrative he had initiated. At the same time Penn decided against "a traditional, all-is-revealed scene at the end." Instead, he self-imposed a challenge: to reveal the culprit entirely in visual action rather than expository dialogue.[145] While the mystery is not ultimately inscrutable, its labyrinthine complexity provokes some bemusement in the tradition of *The Big Sleep*.

The crime at the centre of Sharp's shooting script is the conspiracy of three past and present Hollywood stunt pilots – Iverson, Ziegler, and Ellman – to smuggle ancient Mayan statues from the Yucatán to the Florida Keys. Delly's involvement with these smugglers will lead to her death, while Harry is too blinded by his affection for the macho Ziegler to recognise his complicity.

According to Sharp, Penn decided against centering the conspiracy on drug smuggling,[146] perhaps as a way of distinguishing *his* new Gene Hackman film from *The French Connection* (William Friedkin, 1971). Penn had visited the Yucatán and said he "felt certain that if you were down there shooting a movie you could fly in and out of Mexican air territory without trouble, and move anything and anybody."[147] It's possible Penn and Sharp were inspired by colourful stories about John Huston, a collector of pre-Colombian art, who was said to have smuggled such antiquities into the USA after the Mexican location shoots for *The Treasure of the Sierra Madre* and *The Unforgiven* (1960).[148] UNESCO had officially banned the exportation of valuable antiquities with their World Heritage Convention in late 1972, giving the art smuggling angle a topicality.[149]

The screenplay's backstory is Delly running away from home to join her mechanic boyfriend Quentin on a New

Mexico film set. While there she seduces the macho Ellman, who beats up Quentin when he protests. Delly then finds her way to the Florida Keys to join her former step-father Iverson and his new girlfriend Paula.

Hired by Arlene to find Delly, Harry Moseby follows the trail via the bruised Quentin to the New Mexico film set – where he bonds with Ziegler as a fellow washed-up man of action – and then to Florida, where he finds the missing girl. But before Harry can bring her back to Los Angeles, Delly discovers the plane crash in the waters of the Keys and the partially fish-eaten body of its pilot, Ellman (he had crashed while flying a large statue up from Mexico). Delly suspects that Quentin may have sabotaged Ellman's plane in jealousy, so for now she doesn't reveal the identity of the pilot to Harry. Paula and Iverson pretend to contact the coast guard. Paula seduces Harry to distract him while Iverson seeks (unsuccessfully) to retrieve the loot from the sunken plane.

Shaken by her experience, Delly returns to Los Angeles to live with her mother. Zeigler arranges a job for Delly as a stunt woman. Now reassured by Quentin that he had no role in the plane crash, Delly leaves a message on Harry's answering machine to identify the pilot as Ellman. But Harry does not hear the entirety of the message until after Delly is killed during a dune buggy stunt supervised by Zeigler. Harry suspects Quentin had sabotaged the dune buggy, too. Quentin manages to escape Harry's clutches and flee to Florida. Down in the Keys, Quentin confronts Iverson over Ellman's death, and threatens to inform the Coast Guard. Iverson kills Quentin and dumps his body in a pool of dolphins. Harry arrives soon after, discovers Quentin's body, and fights with Iverson. Iverson dies of his injuries. Paula takes Harry by boat to the site of Ellman's sunken plane, and at dawn she scuba-dives to bring up the loot.

While Paula is underwater, Ziegler arrives in Iverson's seaplane and strafes the boat with fire from a submachine gun. Harry is wounded in the leg and back. A large Mayan statue breaks the surface of the water; Paula rises, too. Ziegler runs down Paula with the alighted plane, but in the process hits the statue. The plane crashes and sinks beneath the boat. Harry and Ziegler make eye contact through the glass bottom as Zeigler drowns inside the cockpit. Harry's boat revolves in circles.

Until its finale, the shooting script depicts Ziegler in largely sympathetic terms through his developing friendship with Harry. The shocking revelation of Zeigler's complicity suggests that he is a manipulative, basically unknowable psychopath. Sharp was never satisfied with the ending, calling it "ineptly contrived."[150] Penn would remain strangely ambivalent about Zeigler and his motivations. "I'm not entirely sure he intended to kill [Delly]," he said. "I think he just meant to topple the car to put her in hospital or something for a brief period so that he could finish up the smuggling operation."[151]

. . .

To bolster what Sharp described as a "threnody for [the] loss of American innocence" after the sixties, the writer used the fate of the Kennedy brothers as one of the film's central metaphors.[152] In the screenplay, Paula first suggests Harry "go find out who shot the President" rather than question her romantic entanglements in Key West.[153] She resumes this theme during the seduction. Apparently *a propos* of nothing, she asks him where he was when Kennedy was shot – "It's one of those questions that everybody knows the answer to," she says. Which Kennedy? Any Kennedy. Harry's memories of the assassinations track a half-decade decline from promising football star to seedy private eye spying on an adulterous couple.

Paula soon admits her underlying reason for suddenly bringing up the Kennedy brothers. The sight of the drowned pilot in his submerged cockpit triggered her memory of the moment she learned about Bobby Kennedy's assassination; the news footage appeared to her "as if everything was happening underwater."[154] Sharp's eventual novelization of his screenplay gives Paula a slightly clearer explanation for this weird misperception of the footage. She says:

> *I was with some guy in a hotel and the television was on and the room was all that blue-cave way and I was watching over this guy's shoulder and it happened and I just started to cry and the guy thought it was because I was coming.*[155]

But Paula's frankly bizarre association of drowning with the Bobby Kennedy assassination seems like a misdirection. Perhaps it is a trace of another element erased in the palimpsest of Sharp's script drafts. Paula's comment actually evokes a third Kennedy tragedy – Chappaquiddick. Late on July 18, 1969, Edward Kennedy, the only surviving brother, accidentally drove his car off a bridge on Chappaquiddick Island in Massachusetts. Mary Jo Kopechne, his 28-year-old passenger, drowned inside the car while Kennedy escaped, fled the scene, and failed to report the accident to police for hours. The scandal and its mysterious circumstances derailed his chances of running for President. Ironically, the accident occurred just days before Apollo 11 landed on the moon, thereby fulfilling the ambitious promise of the slain JFK.

The Dark Tower is preoccupied with drowning – five characters drown or die in water in the shooting script. While Chappaquiddick is never mentioned, the particulars of Kopechne's horrible, claustrophobic drowning inside Kennedy's sinking car seem to haunt the film like the latent content of a dream. This was not without precedent in Penn's work; he had staged a vigilante assassination of a shackled criminal in *The Chase* so that it unambiguously recalled Jack Ruby's murder of Lee Harvey Oswald. The circumstances of Kopechne's death are echoed in *The Dark Tower* on several occasions. Delly dies as the passenger in a stunt car crash which the stunt driver, Zeigler, survives (the shooting script sets this scene in the desert, although that would be changed). Even more powerfully, Zeigler's eventual drowning inside the cockpit of his crashed seaplane – although inspired by an altogether different real-life incident – appears even closer to Kopechne's death, albeit with an ironic reversal of fortune.

3. The First Six Feet
(Summer-Autumn, 1973)

One attraction of the screenplay to its key collaborators was its powerful confession scene.[156] For years Harry Moseby had lied to his wife by claiming he'd once tracked down and spent a week with his long-lost father. In reality, Harry admits to Ellen, he hadn't been able to summon the courage to approach the man he found living in a rooming house on Hibiscus Avenue in Baltimore. From a distance of six feet he watched "this old guy sitting reading the funny pages out of the paper, and his lips were making the words and I just stood there and watched him and then I went away." Ashamed, Harry tells his wife, "I should have jumped... trouble is after the first six feet it's kind of hard to tell whether you're jumping or falling..."[157]

Harry's confession must have resonated with Penn's history of fatherly estrangement. Meanwhile Sharp's quest to track down his relocated birth father had been thwarted because the man was dead. Nevertheless, traces remained. During one visit to Sharp's relocated birth mother in the sixties, Liz Sharp spied an old photograph of a man pinned to a screen. Liz remembers, "I looked at the picture and it came out of my mouth quite naively, 'Oh my God, that's Alan's father!' because he looked identical to Alan. And Alan's mother said, 'No.' But I stole the picture. And it *was* Alan's father."

So who would be right to play Harry Moseby? Everything pointed to Gene Hackman, and not only because both Penn and Sherman had worked with him before. After his supporting role in *Bonnie and Clyde*, Hackman had graduated to leading man status by winning the Academy Award for *The French Connection*. Since then Hackman had taken on diverse roles including a priest in a commercial blockbuster, *The Poseidon Adventure* (Ronald Neame, 1972) and an evil sex-trafficker in the outrageous crime thriller *Prime Cut* (Michael Ritchie, 1972). His box office record was not unblemished. Sanford Production's *Scarecrow*, released in the summer of 1973, failed at the US box office despite critical acclaim. Hackman kept working. In 1973 he had already filmed Francis Ford Coppola's masterful conspiracy thriller *The Conversation* and Jan Troell's western *Zandy's Bride* (both to be released in 1974).

With his height and build, Hackman was physically plausible as the retired football player Harry Moseby. He could project cocky masculinity while simultaneously suggesting depths of sensitivity. He rarely needed to reveal his inner torment through epiphanic outbursts in the Brando-Dean-Clift-Newman tradition. Penn later said of Hackman's performances: "There is an emotional availability that's clearly evident. And there's a stinginess for fear of going into sentimentality which is no part of this man's personality at all."[158]

The screenplay, particularly the confession scene, must have had autobiographical resonances for Hackman as well. In later years, he acknowledged that the childhood trauma of his father's abandonment had made him a better actor, more capable of summoning useful emotions.[159] Penn remarked on "a large dark streak in Hackman's personality, a despairing aspect to him that sometimes verges almost on the tragic. There are constant efforts on his part to find a way to live, and he doesn't succeed at it. He's a man very much damaged by life and who wears the damage. He doesn't deny this. You see it with the camera."[160]

Sharp had not written the part of Moseby with any particular actor in mind. He was surprised by the choice of Hackman because he associated the actor with a working-class persona – evidently a little different from his original conception of Moseby. "He certainly got well away from the whole James Garner tradition of the private eye [in *Marlowe*], which was desirable," Sharp said. "But there were times when I suppose I would have liked him to be just a little more noir romantic than bluff Harry."[161] Otherwise, Sharp was full of praise for the casting: "It's hard for me to imagine who'd be better than Gene Hackman."[162]

. . .

Jennifer Warren, a New York-based stage actress, had recently won a World Theatre Award in Bob Randall and Luke Bower's *6 Rms Riv Vu* (1972). She had co-starred in Robert De Niro's debut film *Sam's Song* (Jordan Leondopoulos, 1969) and worked at the Tyrone Guthrie Theater in Minneapolis.[163] She had been asked to audition in New York for the role of Ellen Moseby. It was her first meeting with Penn, who had seen her onstage.

After the audition Warren felt she was becoming typecast as "the wife" and asked Penn if she could come back to read as Paula. Penn seemed surprised but agreed.[164] Several other actresses were in final consideration for that role, including Warren's friend, Gail Strickland. Paula's delirious monologue about the assassination of Robert Kennedy was used as the audition text, with Gene Lasko reading the part of Harry.[165]

Warren got the gig. She brought to the role the memory of a brief acquaintance with the slain Bobby Kennedy. Warren's first husband had worked with Kennedy in the Bedford Stuyvesant Restoration Foundation, a community development organisation in Brooklyn, which Kennedy had co-founded in 1967. She remembers that after one New York fundraiser for Cesar Chavez, Kennedy had invited Warren and her husband to an intimate dinner at an upscale French restaurant with the socialites Amanda and Carter Burden. The conversation continued late into the evening, a rare opportunity to get to know the man who would seek the democratic nomination for President.

But that night there was a small problem. Warren and her husband presently worked as janitors in their Greenwich Village apartment building in exchange for a discount on their rent. One unbreakable rule of this arrangement was that the building's hallways had to be mopped by midnight. Duty called.

"After the main course and before dessert, we said, 'you'll have to excuse us – we have to leave for an earlier commitment'." Warren remembers with a laugh. "Yeah, to wash the hallways before midnight! That moment always stuck with me."

Bobby Kennedy was assassinated soon after that dinner. Reading Sharp's screenplay, Warren was in a good position to empathise with Paula's Kennedy trauma. "Those iterations were close to me, too," she remembers.[166]

The Canadian actress Susan Clark had studied at London's Royal Academy of Dramatic Art and at the Stella Adler Academy and was presently under contract as a studio player – among the last of a vanishing species in a changing Hollywood. In recent years she had co-starred with a number of Hollywood's leading men including Clint Eastwood, Robert Redford, James Garner, and Burt Lancaster. She had previously worked with Hackman in the golfing drama *Banning* (1967).

Early during the summer of 1973, at the same time as the Senate Watergate Committee hearings, Clark was rehearsing for S. N. Behrman's *The Second Man* at the Williamstown Theater Festival in Massachusetts. Invited to audition for the role of Ellen Moseby, Clark rented a car to drive to Penn's house in nearby Stockbridge. The audition was a relaxed conversation rather than a formal reading of the part. "He put me at his ease in his living room, and we talked about the theatre, and he talked about Stella Adler, and we talked. We had some kind of common ground." The audition was a success. Clark's contract with Universal meant she would be simply loaned out to Warners for the duration of the filming.[167]

The role of Delly went to Melanie Griffith, the young daughter of Hitchcock's former leading lady, Tippi Hedren. At the time Hedren was operating the Shambala lion sanctuary at a ranch in Acton, California, alongside her present husband, Noel Marshall, about to find great success as the executive producer of *The Exorcist* (1973).[168]

Griffith had grown up in the company of African lions. She turned sixteen in the summer of 1973. Her boyfriend, the actor Don Johnson, had encouraged her to work as a model. When she was unexpectedly called to audition at Warner Brothers Studios, she turned up under the impression it was a modelling interview. The audition had come about because her friend, the model Karen Lamm, had also auditioned for Delly; when Lamm did not get the role, she recommended Griffith.[169]

But Griffith was not keen to follow her mother's profession. She had neither acting training nor experience. Nevertheless, she met with Penn, who gave her pages of the screenplay to memorize. She rehearsed at home with Johnson and returned to Warner Brothers. She recalled that Penn "made me pound on the chair to get really mad – I didn't know how to do anything then – I just pretended I was that person, and all of a sudden I got the job. It was like, "Wow, I'm co-starring in a movie with Gene Hackman!"[170]

. . .

The cast was rounded out with Edward Binns as Zeigler, Kenneth Mars as Nick, Janet Ward as Arlene, and the young James Woods as Quentin. Susan Clark remembers that Harris Yulin was particularly keen to work with Arthur Penn, and she supported his casting for the important role of her character's lover, Marty Heller. A Los Angeles-born theatre actor who had already done a lot of television work, Yulin had acted with Clark earlier that year in Burt Lancaster's detective film *The Midnight Man* (released 1974).

In September the almost-complete cast assembled at Warner Brothers in Burbank for about ten days of rehearsals and improvisations. Clark remembers Penn had to fight for the luxury of this rehearsal time. A small soundstage at the studio had been mocked up in a rough approximation of the planned sets. "They had taped the rehearsal space [floor] and had pieces of furniture that we walked around," Clark remembers. "Of course, it never matches."

The rehearsal period was largely focused on getting the script into filmable shape. Sharp had finished a complete draft of the shooting script on Monday, September 17th, evidently just in time for the rehearsals at Warner Bros Studios. While this draft would be the foundation of what was filmed, many of its pages would be replaced in the coming weeks. Sharp and Penn were still catching up after the imposed delay of the three-and-a-half month writers' strike.

Nevertheless, Jennifer Warren remembers the assembled cast was unanimous in its enthusiasm. "It's not often that you go into a shoot and within the first couple of days everybody is telling everybody how much they're excited about the script," Jennifer Warren now reflects. "I figure if you have that four times in your life, you're lucky. And everybody knew it was one of those."[171]

Sharp struck up fast friendships with both Clark and Warren. He gave each of them copies of *A Green Tree in Gedde*. "He was an amazing character," Clark remembers. "I thought he was terrific. He had a whole bunch of kids. He was fascinating. I learned more about him reading his novel." Warren remembers Sharp fondly as a "Fozzie Bear" with his "red beard and moustache."[172] He was "a great storyteller and passionate about his work," with an uncommon aptitude for writing female characters. He told Warren that Paula was his "spokesperson" in the screenplay. So why hadn't he written the film from her point of view? He told her it was a commercial decision.[173]

Penn helped his actors develop their characters in advance of the filming. Clark remembers, "He would ask questions – 'Why do you think you're doing this? Where does this scene take you?' [...] Arthur was in the Hitchcock School. He'd say, 'This is what we have rehearsal for. Now you go home and do your homework. And I will keep us on the straight and narrow of where we're supposed to go with the film'."

Almost immediately Warren was dismayed by Hackman's curmudgeonly reluctance to rehearse and improvise. She remembers him groaning, "Oh, I forgot. Arthur does this." Warren, on the other hand, was "hot to trot. I wanted to work, to do it, and he's complaining. So when we started to rehearse a scene he made some humorous crack instead of the line, which made me even crankier. So then I started back at him – 'That's really smart talk, huh? That's supposed to be humorous?' We started our relationship on that tone," she laughs.[174]

While rehearsals went on, *The Conversation* was in post-production on the lot. Editor Walter Murch had substantially reorganised the structure of the film in the absence of its writer and director, Francis Ford Coppola, who was days away from beginning to shoot the ambitious *Godfather Part II* (1974). Hackman invited Warren to join him at his first dialogue looping session.

"It was the first time he saw it or himself in it," she remembers.

In *The Conversation* Hackman played Harry Caul, an introverted surveillance technician who hides behind the anonymity of thick glasses, a moustache, and a grey transparent raincoat. Now, in the darkness of the dubbing suite, Hackman was disturbed to see himself on screen.

"'Oh shit,'" Hackman said to Warren.

"'What?'"

"'I look just like my father.'"

"That was really hard on him," Warren remembers. "Then he went right into the looping session. It was a fight, but he was miraculous at it… Oh, that was hard. Gene liked the film but hated himself in it. That's not what he wanted to see. Obviously that's what he thought of, but he must have made those choices subliminally."

. . .

Presumably typing through the night, Sharp worked hard on script revisions immediately after completing the draft of September 17, evidently to take advantage of what insights were emerging day by day from rehearsals. Sharp made targeted passes to tweak specific themes, characters, and plot threads.[175]

Nevertheless, with filming about to begin in Los Angeles, there wasn't enough time to get the screenplay into a completely satisfactory state. It was during rehearsals that Sharp became disenchanted with Penn as a collaborator. He "realised we weren't working very well." The problems, Sharp believed, "stemmed from Arthur's uncertainty about the kind of film he was going to make." According to Sharp,

Harry Moseby (Gene Hackman) and Ellen Moseby (Susan Clark)

"When we finally got up to the wire to make the movie, it took me quite a while to actually accept the fact that Arthur didn't know what he wanted to do."[176]

4. The Dark Tower
(Autumn-Winter, 1973)

Penn's preparations for filming *The Dark Tower* did not include storyboarding. By sketching in advance every shot, essentially pre-editing the film on paper, he could have restricted filming to a minimum of camera set-ups. But that wasn't his work method. To allow himself the maximum freedom during editing he shot extensive coverage, obtaining complete takes of each scene from a multitude of framings and angles. He said that he liked to set up "one aspect towards one person, as we shoot a wide shot, a medium shot, a close shot, and a very close shot; and then we turn around and go in the other direction."[177] Penn said he "always [knows] more or less how my shots are going to cut" and filmed "with a certain style of editing in mind that demands a lot of material.... with lots of shots it's possible to work on the film's rhythm, to change it, to speed it up."[178] Except for action sequences featuring special effects that were expensive to repeat, he did not employ multiple cameras.[179]

Penn's approach alarmed executives at Warner Brothers, but Robert Sherman remained confident. "Arthur got all the coverage in the world, and yet he stayed on schedule," Sherman remembered:

> *We were shooting a scene in a kitchen that we rented in the Valley and there was a neon beer sign over the refrigerator. Arthur wanted to get a master, over-the-shoulder, and then he wanted to get a medium close-up, and then a close-up, all the same angle. I got a call from Warners saying 'What the fuck is he doing? Has he got a deal with Miller beer?' I said, 'Read the script. That's about a ten second scene. He just wants to make sure he's got the performance right. You're fixing on the neon sign and he's fixing on the actor.' And I never got that call again. It's astonishing. [Penn] is my hero.*[180]

Sharp was less convinced. He interpreted Penn's approach to filming *The Dark Tower* as another manifestation of the indecision he'd revealed during the still-ongoing screenwriting process. He would come to describe Penn as "a guy whose sensitivity prevents him from reaching final conclusions – he's Hamletian, in that sense."[181]

Penn's cinematographer was Bruce Surtees, who had recently come to prominence shooting films directed by Don Siegel and Clint Eastwood. Eastwood later praised Surtees' willingness to risk "shooting with low-light contrast. He was always looking to improve shots, and he could do a lot with little equipment in a very short time."[182] Much of *The Dark Tower* would be shot outdoors, and the locations in Los Angeles and Florida – two conventional settings for the detective genre – provided a diversity of dazzling days and noirish nights.

The streets of Los Angeles, the classic beat of Raymond Chandler's Philip Marlowe and Ross MacDonald's Lew Archer, provided visually distinct exteriors that emphasise the characters' relative functions in the society of the city. Harry's office was filmed at 4310 Beverly Boulevard in a drab neighbourhood north of what was later known as Koreatown. In the main title sequence Harry drives west on Sunset Boulevard past the legendary Schwab's Drugstore (close to the Sharps' home on Marmont Lane across from the equally legendary Chateau Marmont) to Ellen Moseby's upmarket gallery, the vaguely fascist-sounding Falanga Antiques.

The interior of the antiques showroom was a set. The scene at Falanga was scheduled for Susan Clark's first day of filming. "I was terrified, and Arthur saw this," Clark remembers. Penn gave her a distracting bit of action to focus her attention in the scene. "He said, 'No, don't look up – I want you to find a piece of paper under that pile. That's the whole action." So that took me away from the nerves. All that paper shuffling."

Harry and Ellen's house was filmed at 3221 Berry Drive in Studio City, an affluent neighbourhood in the San Fernando Valley. Several scenes were shot on the back lot and in one of the projection rooms of Warner Brothers Studios in Burbank. Many of the other Los Angeles locations were within easy reach of the studio. Moody night shots depict Harry driving through the Burbank streets. The Magnolia Theatre, where Harry spies on Ellen and her lover Marty Heller coming out of an Eric Rohmer film, stood at 4403

Marty Heller (Harris Yulin) and Arlene Iverson (Janet Ward)

West Magnolia Boulevard. Harry's much-quoted comparison of Rohmer's films to "like watching painting dry," was originally directed at the work of another French New Wave *auteur*, Claude Chabrol. Penn decided the comment "was in no way applicable to Chabrol" and swapped the love story *Le Boucher* (1969) for Rohmer's talky, philosophical *My Night At Maud's* (1969).[183]

Harris Yulin was an unusual casting choice for Heller. Physically much smaller than the athletic Harry, he upsets the kind of conventional cuckolding scenario the macho Harry can understand – as when Ellman, the dominant alpha male, has sex with Delly and beats up the weaselly Quentin. Ellen's affair with Heller challenges Harry's sense of machismo, and as if to amplify the disruption even further, Yulin plays Heller with a limp.

Heller lives in a small but upmarket beachfront apartment. Penn filmed the exteriors and interiors at 25370 Malibu Road. The apartment's decorations – the art-crowded walls, the books, the hi-fi playing cello music, the wine and cheese and grapes – immediately distinguish Heller's preoccupations from Harry's. But the fisheye lenses refracting the Pacific Ocean horizon matches the lens in Harry's attic window – a subtle way of saying 'Ellen was here.' In a later scene Penn and Surtees filmed back through this extreme wide-angle lens *into* the apartment, creating a surreal distortion within a context of ostensible realism.

Janet Ward played the washed-up former B-movie ingénue, Arlene Iverson. Ward was an Actors Studio alumnus who had performed on live television. Her feature film experience was limited to two pictures by Sidney Lumet, *Fail Safe* (1964) and *The Anderson Tapes* (1971). The script

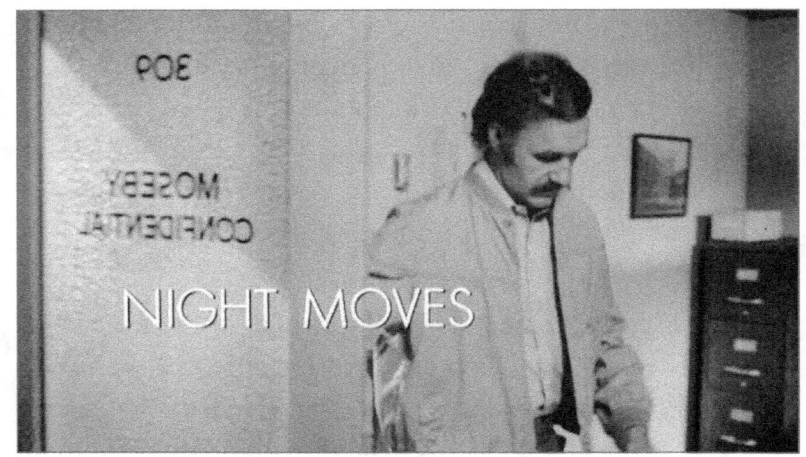

Harry's office

gives Arlene's address as 3740 Sunset Plaza, but this was amended when spoken on screen to 1536, presumably for continuity with the number visible on the house that was chosen for the exteriors. That house was not actually on Sunset Plaza but in the same neighbourhood at 1536 Rising Glen. The house's interior and backyard, with its spectacular view of the hills beyond its swimming pool, does not match this house's location and was shot elsewhere.

Penn took advantage of an NFL game between the Los Angeles Rams and the Dallas Cowboys at the Los Angeles Memorial Coliseum on Sunday, October 14, 1973. Hackman and two other actors, Edward Binns and Kenneth Mars, were filmed in the crowd of spectators during the game, although Penn filmed the first part of the scene, the conversation in the tunnel, when the stadium was empty.[184]

While the Los Angeles exteriors help reinforce the characters and their place in society, the interior sets are much less successful. George Jenkins had designed stage sets for Penn's *Two for the Seesaw* and *The Miracle Worker* (both 1959), and then for his films of *The Miracle Worker* and *Mickey One*. But something went wrong this time. The sets are one of the weakest aspects of the film. Many are rudimentary and surprisingly artless for a large budget studio picture. Harry's office is the main exception: its venetian blinds and waiting annex partitioned by pebbled glass recall the offices of any number of movie PIs, although the supposedly anti-technology Harry has a "Code-A-Phone 700" answering machine instead of a sassy secretary. The set was decorated with filing cabinets, maps of Los Angeles, an old football trophy, a dart board and a

Falanga Antiques and Nick's Office

coffee urn. Nevertheless, the walls are flimsy and noticeably shake when Harry closes the door.

The other constructed interiors look cheap and perfunctory, with little thought to their function in the story. Falanga Antiques, intended to be an upmarket showroom, is cluttered with seemingly random curios and is gloomily underlit. The set for Nick's agency – the "information factory,"[185] as Harry calls it with disapproval – is completely inadequate for its dramatic purpose. The shooting script describes "a largish modern office, chrome and leather chairs, hessian on the walls, modern prints."[186] Nick's office is supposed to make a professional, technologically advanced contrast to Harry's old-fashioned, generically conventional HQ. The set as realised does not in any way communicate Nick's success in the detective business. On the contrary, the cramped office looks even more run-down than Harry's. The computerization of the business is vaguely suggested by a primitive print-out of a *Playboy* centrefold tacked to the wall, but with its ineptly light-reflective wood panelling and generic furniture, Nick's office seems quickly improvised. Neither the sets nor the cinematography in these two scenes rise above the standards of a contemporary *NBC Mystery Movie*.

The scene in Nick's office is weak in other ways. Sharp used the scene to present important expositional dialogue about the rising value of Mexican antiquities, "specially now that the Mexicans have got their backs up about their art treasures being ripped off," explains Nick, who is a collector[187] (on this dreadfully inept set, Nick's supposedly valuable statues are housed in the most utilitarian of glass display cabinets). The conversation might seem to hint that

Nick is himself involved in the Mexican artefact-smuggling conspiracy of the stunt pilots, but that is a red herring – at least by the final draft of the shooting script. The coincidence of Ellen's profession (an antiques dealer) and the theme of artefact smuggling is similarly suggestive but ultimately irrelevant.

Perhaps in early drafts, while Sharp still planned a whodunit with no solution, he had intentionally paraded a range of plausible suspects to the audience. The shooting script is something of a palimpsest of shifting intentions, never finalised to Sharp's satisfaction, and traces of this earlier conception may not have been entirely erased during the extensive rewrites. But it is puzzling why Sharp did not establish the Mexican antiquities theme during Harry's dialogue with Ellen's gay co-worker Charles at Falanga Antiques, where the expositional information could have arisen much more naturally from the setting.

In the shooting script the scene in Nick's office is followed by a conversation inside his agency's 'Computer Room'. Nick tries to lure Harry to work for him. "We still need somebody in Data Analysis," Nick says. "Somebody who can smell the dirt among the digits." Computers, Nick acknowledges, are "dumb but they're quick." Harry makes a quip about their similarity to football players, and Nick concludes "You're a dinosaur. You're not evolving with the times."[188] Although nicely reinforcing the theme of Harry's antiquated detective methods in a technologically advanced society, this scene did not make the final cut. It may not have been shot. Kenneth Mars, a talented comic actor specialising in outlandish foreign accents, proved a poor choice for the straight role of Nick. Eating and drinking his way through his two surviving scenes, Mars plays Nick in a strange, superficial mode of cheerful detachment. His dialogue was also clumsily post-synchronized.

Transcending the several artistic failures of the Los Angeles shoot was Gene Hackman. His performance was without a trace of vanity. Sharp was very happy: "Lines that had been written just to get you from one line to the next line came alive with him."[189] Faced with the weaker scenes, Hackman was able to "to generate energy out of nothing."[190] Hackman gave Harry a signature parting gesture – he forms a pistol with his hand and fires a shot. For the role Hackman wore a moustache similar to Sharp's, and only after the filming did the writer realise that Hackman had "constructed many of the character's mannerisms on his observation of me."[191] The autobiographical hints were in the script: Sharp was about to turn forty on January 12, 1974; a piece of dialogue in the shooting script reveals that forty-year-old Harry shares a birthday with his creator.[192]

For Susan Clark, working with Hackman was "scary. He was so intense that it was frightening, and so really good at his job. I don't know if it was my inexperience or the intensity of the whole film – it was stunning but it wasn't fun... Gene was in an unhappy marital situation and I was getting a divorce. So we were both quite fragile."

Among the most challenging scenes was Harry's confession, shot on a studio set representing the couple's bedroom. Hackman performed the monologue with his customary understatement. The vivid detail about Harry's father sitting on a park bench isn't in the shooting script and was probably ad-libbed. Harry admits he didn't have the courage to approach his father and smothers his vulnerability under smiles and weak jokes. Sherman remembered that Penn "ran Gene Hackman through the mill on that scene where he's talking about his father" and eventually "Gene had to say, 'I can't do any more.'"[193]

Clark observes that although Hackman may have been "emotionally available to an audience" he was "not emotionally available to another character... I think that's one of the reasons why Arthur pushed our scenes to the heights of disagreement [...] I think we did forty-two takes, Gene Hackman and I half-naked in bed. Arthur sat on the floor with his face right beside the lens shooting up, and he would pound the floor saying, 'No, no, no! He's dying, he's drowning. You have to save him!' And Gene Hackman was six inches from me saying 'what do we do now?' But he just shrugged. He'd worked with Arthur before, and he knew that he had this absolutely specific idea of what he wanted in the scene. At the end of it our respective dressers came with warmed terrycloth robes to cover us and a big glass of brandy which we both needed."

Clark enjoyed performing the scene of the marital argument in the kitchen, another studio set. "At one moment of frustration I leaned up overhead and smacked all the pots and pans and they made a huge clattering noise. That startled Hackman and took the scene in a different direction. At the end of it he said, 'You got to the pots and pans before me. I planned on doing it but you got there first'."

But there was little levity when the cameras stopped filming. "There was no small talk with Gene Hackman," Clark says. "He would disappear into his dressing room, and I would go into my dressing room, and there was no hanging out. [...] I think it was partly what was going on in his personal life as well as the pressure that he felt from Arthur. And just the man himself. Very serious. He was a very serious actor."

Clark found the experience of working with Penn challenging but enormously rewarding. "My memory of *Night Moves* is one of being off-balance, but I never attributed that to the film. In fact, I think Arthur helped me greatly by giving me the opportunity to use the confusions and memories and whatever I was living through. And there it was written on the page, a nice merging of life and art.... He was a wonderful person and a talented guy. It was such a joy to work with him. But he was also really tough."

Clark ultimately delivered a sympathetic performance in a challenging role – an unfaithful wife who, when exposed as an adulteress, refuses to allow her husband to wallow in cuckolded self-pity.

By 11 October Sharp had rewritten the airport scene between Harry and Ellen. Sharp's original version of their farewell was not supposed to convey much hope for their marriage. Sharp's eventual novelization of his script preserves the substance of his original scene. Ellen accuses Harry of having "tunnel vision, you only see straight ahead. I suppose I would like to have been what you saw at the end of your tunnel, but I'm not.... Well, you better go down that tunnel and see what it is. And I'll go down mine and when we come out on the other side maybe we can look around, maybe we'll come out in the same place."[194]

Robert Sherman remembered how Penn and Sharp diverged in their attitudes to marriage, and that this difference seemed to play out in their tussle over Harry and Ellen's farewell. While Penn was a committed family man,

> *Alan had had a number of marriages and relationships, and he took a more existential view of it: this is it, it's not gonna work, we're moving on. Reconciling polar extremes like that is difficult [...] It's something that should have been worked out between Arthur and Alan before we got there.*[195]

Under pressure from Penn, Sharp rewrote the airport scene. The adage Ellen ultimately offers to Harry – "If you don't go, you can't come back" – had been a recurring line in *A Green Tree in Gedde*. Sharp didn't like reworking the scene that way. "She sounds like a good little missus, and that wasn't for me," he said.[196] But that is how it was filmed at Los Angeles Airport.

Susan Clark believes the rewritten scene left the fate of the relationship appropriately ambiguous in a way that reflected the discord between Penn and Sharp. "Arthur was married for a very long time and had, I would say, a more North American view of marriage which is that you don't ditch it when things get rough. You wait it out and if it's meant to be it will come back on track. I think Alan Sharp had a more European view. It seemed to me that we left it very open, vague. You could think either way. It was left for the audience to decide."

The company would be back in California in December to wrap up. They shot the Los Angeles driving scenes in the main title sequence as well as the exterior scenes set in New Mexico, including the plane stunt that introduces Marv Ellman, played by Anthony Costello with a braying laugh in a broad caricature of an arrogant stud. This was shot at the Indian Dunes film ranch in Valencia.

It is probable that Delly's death in a stunt car crash was filmed at this late stage. At least until the end of October, that sequence was still intended to be shot in the desert. A dune buggy driven by Zeigler would crash into a gully, and Delly's death captured from multiple angles by a fictional film crew. But Penn, in collaboration with a stunt driver, reworked the idea. The desert setting was abandoned in favour of a Hollywood studio back lot. Sharp was not enthused by the change. As Sharp put it, "The stunt man had a gimmick which he was dying to use. It was a cannon placed in the back of a car, which fires a shot into the ground and by doing so, throws the car over onto its side." The result was outside the realm of plausibility, "so spectacular it was unusable". The ultimate solution would be to keep the moment of the accident off camera; only the bloody aftermath of the crash would be shown, captured *verité* style on 16 mm by film students.[197]

During filming, Penn evidently found it necessary to add an early glimpse of Zeigler's capacity for sudden violence: the scene in a New Mexico bar was revised to include an incident in which he assaults a drunken young dancer who spills his drink. Sharp's novelization does not include that incident but it more frequently emphasises Zeigler's machismo, a quality Harry uncritically admires.

. . .

Florida had become a familiar landscape of the crime genre, and it shouldn't be surprising that some of the settings of Huston's *Key Largo* reappeared in *The Dark Tower* in gentle homage. It is also likely that Penn and Sharp were aware of Thomas McGuane's new novel *Ninety-Two in the Shade*, a cock-eyed comedy of drugs, booze, sex, madness, and death in Key West. It was published in the summer of 1973. In fact, a colourful line from McGuane's novel – "I'm the kind of guy who'd fuck a brushpile on the chance there was a snake in it"[198] – re-appeared almost unchanged in *The Dark Tower*.

In pre-production Penn and Sharp had gone location scouting in Florida. It was the longest period of time the two had yet spent together. For Sharp it was a return to the scene of his original inspiration, but the Keys did not impress Penn as amenable for filming. At Islamorada, south of Key Largo, Penn was disappointed to find an over-developed landscape that failed to match the wild frontier of his imagination. "Christ, it looks like Red Bank, New Jersey," he was reported as saying.[199] According to Sharp, Penn was also wary of the logistical challenges of recording live dialogue in unavoidable proximity to U.S. Route 1.[200] (McGuane was shortly to direct his own middling adaptation of *Ninety-Two in the Shade* on location in Key West, sound problems be damned.)

Finally Penn opted to shoot *The Dark Tower* on the Florida Gulf Coast. The bulk of the locations would be on or near Sanibel Island in Lee County, an effective double for the Keys. In 1973 Sanibel was on the cusp of incorporating as a city and enacting strict preservation laws to prevent the unhindered development of the commercial tourist industry. Warner Bros built several small sets in the vicinity of the island.

Penn and Hackman arrived on Sanibel late on Sunday, October 28th. The film company, in Florida for five weeks, numbered almost seventy-five.[201] Gene Hackman's brother Richard served as his stand-in. The cast and crew lodged at Sanibel Moorings, a hotel on the beach[202] – substantially more luxurious than the fictitious Gulf Shores, the run-down complex of waterside cabins where Tom Iverson and Paula live. Chef Sergio Roscoe put in sixteen-hour shifts six days a week to feed the company from his mobile food van. The local press eagerly reported that Hackman liked Roscoe's scrambled eggs, Penn ate yogurt and apples, Warren ate cheese, and Griffith was a vegetarian. The logistical challenges included bringing in a thousand pounds of ice every day from the nearby city of Fort Meyers.[203]

Sharp was also on location for most of the filming; he left his wife and young children back in Los Angeles and had several short-lived affairs during the production.[204] Although in later years he did not recall "any particularly riotous evenings" on Sanibel,[205] Melanie Griffith remembered his presence differently: "Alan Sharp. Yeah, he was crazy. He was the writer. He was there. He was wild, drinking a lot and having a good time, being very emotional."[206]

During the first week Penn filmed what was reported in the press to be a car chase north of Tarpon Bay and on the causeway between the mainland and Sanibel. This mysterious car chase was not in the shooting script.[207] They encountered some minor resistance gaining permission from the local authorities but it was soon overcome.[208] By the second week filming was underway at Punta Rassa, back across the causeway on the mainland, doubling for the Keys' Islamorada. The company built a marina with a dolphin pool.[209] The set and Penn's framing resembled the marina in the opening sequence of *Key Largo*.

Key Largo and *Night Moves*

Jennifer Warren was made up to appear deeply tanned.[210] She remembers that on her first day on location, Hackman was complaining about Penn's extensive coverage: "Arthur likes to do *every frigging set-up*," he groaned, "and we have to do *every frigging set-up*."[211] A consequence of the many takes was a lack of sunlight continuity from shot to shot in a number of the outdoor scenes around Sanibel.

It was Warren's idea to read some of her lines in a voice imitative of Humphrey Bogart, thereby making fun of Harry-the-private-detective – a clever inspiration in a script full of references to the iconic actor. Warren remembers that Penn was mildly sceptical of the Bogart voice, but her justification was that:

Paula's such a put-down artist about the rest of the world that's gone to hell... When I'm in bad trouble in my life, I start to get funnier. And I think that was the same kind of take I had on her. The worse things got, the more humorous you try to make them.

Warren found Hackman to be "a miraculous actor. Seemingly without any preparation, he's just there, in touch with the truth."[212] Their dialogue together was playful and flirtatious. Paula recounts an urban legend about "blind albino shit-eating alligators" that had overrun the New York City sewage system (Sharp had already used the story in his novel *The Wind Shifts*). When Harry doubts its veracity, Paula delivers a line that becomes a motif in the screenplay (Harry repeats it to Ellen): "the truth is a lie that hasn't been found out yet." The recurring line would be eliminated in the editing room.[213]

Penn directing Jennifer Warren at Punta Rassa (*The Day of the Director*)

The filmmakers were not exempt from routine promotional duties during filming. The shy Hackman was finally cornered by a local reporter at Punta Rassa. Fidgeting with his wedding ring, he made platitudinous statements about Penn, spoke of missing the theatre, and his own vague desire to direct a film.[214] Sharp was also interviewed and explained the origins of the screenplay in his visit to the Keys five years earlier.[215]

Warner Brothers sent a documentary crew to the location to film Penn directing the first Harry-Paula meeting at the dolphin pool as well as the choreography of a brief fight scene between Harry and some local "conchs" defending Delly.[216]

The last major role, Tom Iverson, had now been cast. John Crawford was a capable if unspectacular actor with a James Stewart drawl. He had appeared in *The Poseidon Adventure* and had co-written Sam Peckinpah's gentle comic western *The Ballad of Cable Hogue* (1970). Overweight, Crawford played Iverson as a grizzled seafarer. His casting was a little disruptive for Jennifer Warren. "Since I hadn't met him, I had made a substitution in my head for what that guy would be like. In my head Iverson was more like Spencer Tracy when he was older – white hair, avuncular, you really liked him," she remembers with a laugh. "And then I was on set and John Crawford appeared. He wasn't like Spencer Tracy. I said, 'Well, she's a lot lower on the pecking scale than I thought.'"[217]

Penn described his approach to directing actors:

I get to know their personal lives, and then I ask them to draw on that every once in a while; a lot of it is

Paula (Jennifer Warren) and Delly (Melanie Griffith)

confidential. But I try to find parallels in their own lives to the sort of situations they're experiencing in the film, and to give them a point of recognition so that they don't go into a completely alien situation.[218]

In later years Hackman praised Penn's technique:

The kind of thing that Arthur does, and a lot of good directors do, doesn't feel like direction. It feels like your uncle is there to support you [...] People have an idea that actors need a lot of direction. Maybe some people do. I tend to go the other way. If I get too much direction then I'm thinking only of that. I'm not thinking about this effective memory that I'm going to do. And that's very important to me.[219]

Warren, however, was surprised by Penn's minimal direction of her performance, odd for a director with a reputation as an actor's director:

He never said much to me, which always struck me as strange. We never talked about the scene or the script. I'd say, 'Any thoughts, Arthur?' And he'd say, 'No, no.' But the one thing he did say was, 'you can trust me. If something is going wrong, if something is off, I will see it and I will tell you'. And that you did believe. But why he didn't go further, being able to talk about the scene, always surprised me.

Warren doesn't recall Penn discussing the screenplay's Kennedy references during the shooting, nor any of his personal history with the Kennedy brothers. He didn't mention it as they were walking to the set to shoot the love scene. When she asked Penn for guidance in that difficult scene, he gave advice that she found unhelpful:

> He said, "Do it for your father." The wrong scene to say that about. He knew my father had died when I was young, and he knew that loss was important, but to then put that together? I just had to erase that from my mind. What a dumb-ass thing to say. It really threw me because he is supposed to be the actor's director and he didn't know what to say to me before we shot that scene. What he came out with was wrong. So I just thought, "Don't think about that, put that aside."

It was a demanding semi-nude sex scene during which she had to deliver a page-long monologue about her early sexual experiences and her disillusionment after the assassination of Bobby Kennedy. Warren remembers that "all of a sudden every Warner Brothers executive" turned up on set "to check out my makeup." Nevertheless, she maintained her focus:

> I worked on that scene more than anything else in the whole movie because I knew if I didn't feel some sense of privacy it was not going to be good. So I was very proud of myself that I was able to keep that privacy, keep my substitutions, and keep on track.[220]

Sharp praised Warren's unusual but emotionally powerful performance of this unconventional scene.[221] The editing of this love scene would come to be a major point of contention, pitting Penn against Sharp and Warren.

. . .

Melanie Griffith, who had still not graduated from high school, had a tutor on set. She was completely new to acting. Penn advised her to read the script and invent a life for the character of Delly. "Make a life for her?" Griffith remembered thinking. "What does that mean? There's not a real *her*. I didn't understand."

On her first day Griffith was filmed undressing behind a clothesline at Gulf Shores. She remembered:

> *I didn't know how to move my body and walk and talk at the same time. I was so scared. It was my first time in front of the camera and the crew, and I was taking my shirt off and I was nervous, and there's Gene Hackman, and all these other things going on, and I remember Arthur getting below the camera line and moving my hips so that I would actually move my body a little bit. And then, all of a sudden, something happened, and it was sort of magical, and it was just easy. Gene made it very easy for me, and fun, and I loved it. It changed immediately.*

Penn sometimes had to resort to tricks to get the appropriate emotional reaction from Griffith. During the scene following Delly's nightmare, when she is comforted by Harry, Penn filmed Hackman first. When it came time to film her own close-ups, Griffith was no longer able to cry. She recalled:

> *Arthur, right in front of me, saying to the make-up guy, "do you have those drops that they use for actors who can't pull up the emotion?" And the guy said, "I dunno, I have 'em, but I haven't had to use 'em in so many years." At that, I immediately burst into tears – that I was going to be the first actress that had to use those in so many years. That made me cry, and Arthur said, "Roll camera."*[222]

Griffith's performance met the considerable challenges of this complicated role – a testament to Penn's skilful direction and her innate talent.

. . .

By the third week on Sanibel the atmosphere had soured. The company was working long and arduous shifts, some of them night shoots which began at 8 pm. The crew had to douse themselves in mosquito repellent. "We've used up sixteen cases of this stuff since we've been here," complained a sound engineer.[223] In light of the island's limited diversions and underdeveloped amenities, the crew began to call it Sani-Flush.[224] Sharp remembered, "There was a fair amount of grousing that began to come up, but I wasn't a real insider on it."[225]

A general break-down in communications put a wedge between Penn and his crew. Warren told an on-set journalist, "Arthur and the actors are in an absolutely separate realm. What does everybody else know? They can't even see what's happening sometimes." Hackman acknowledged the difficulty of bringing technicians onto the picture after the start of shooting: "They may or may not have read the script."

Mistakes were made. One day there was a continuity error in Gene Hackman's make-up in a scene shot out on Pine Island Sound, just off Sanibel, in a thirty-two-foot glass-bottomed boat called the *Point of View*. Harry was supposed to be wearing the cuts and bruises from his brutal fight with Iverson (a scene which had not yet been shot). Make-up artist Bob Stein had merely followed an instruction to make Hackman appear "dirty and wet." Hackman had to be brought back to shore and duly made up again to re-shoot the scene, but by the time he was ready the sun was gone – a "$20,000 misunderstanding", in the words of one crew member.[226]

The movie was to end in despair. To offset the optimistic rewrite of the Los Angeles airport scene – "if you don't go, you can't come back" – Sharp wanted to eliminate any chance of a reconciliation between Harry and his wife. Harry should die by the bullet like all of his other screen heroes to date.[227] However, this was a denouement he wasn't entirely able to achieve (Harry's ultimate fate is unresolved). Sharp's unrelenting noirness had by now probably become too much for Penn, who would introduce a number of other small changes, mostly in post-production, to lighten what was still one of the bleakest films of the era.

Zeigler's botched attack by seaplane on Harry and Paula proved difficult and expensive to film. The sequence: the seaplane appears in the skies and fires upon defenceless Harry in the *Point of View* as Paula dives for the sunken Mexican statue. The seaplane lands on the water. As Paula and the loot break the surface, the seaplane violently runs her down before accidentally crashing into the Mexican statue. Poised over the glass-bottom, Harry watches the plane sink beneath the boat. The drowning pilot, he sees, is Joey Zeigler.

The sequence must have been partly inspired by the famous crop-dusting plane attack in Alfred Hitchcock's *North By Northwest* (1959) – actor Edward Binns had actually appeared in a small role in another scene in Hitchcock's film – and it was also a reworking of the final shoot-out on the boat at the conclusion of *Key Largo*, itself an unofficial lift from Hemingway's *To Have and Have Not*.

The 1958 newsreel of the accidental drowning of Commander J. D. Russell.

Sharp acknowledged another influence on the sequence – a disturbing newsreel that documented the accidental death of Commander J. D. Russell of the British Royal Navy in 1958.[228] In an attempt to land a Scimitar on the aircraft carrier H.M.S. Victorious, an arrester wire broke and the plane rolled off the carrier and into the sea. The pilot was unable to remove the cockpit canopy and drowned as the plane sank.

Warren had undergone scuba diving training in a New York City pool. "Being that I'm slightly claustrophobic, it was a real act of courage." Although a stuntwoman had been hired to perform in certain shots, Warren ended up doing the work herself.

The red tide had come to Sanibel a week before we were going out on the water. The red tide makes for hundreds of thousands of dead fish, so the sharks come in and feed... The stunt double waits till we get to the water and she says to Arthur, 'I'm not diving. It's too dangerous. The sharks are everywhere because of the red tide.' There we are: the boat, the follow boat, the whole crew... So guess what happened next? Arthur says, "Jennifer, our stunt double is too scared to go into the water so would you mind jumping in? We'll have a watchboat on the other side, and if they see any activity they'll call cut." Then I found out afterwards that they did see activity but we had just called action and they were scared to call a cut. I don't think the shark could see me either. You couldn't see your hand in front of your face in there. It was so murky with dead fish floating around.[229]

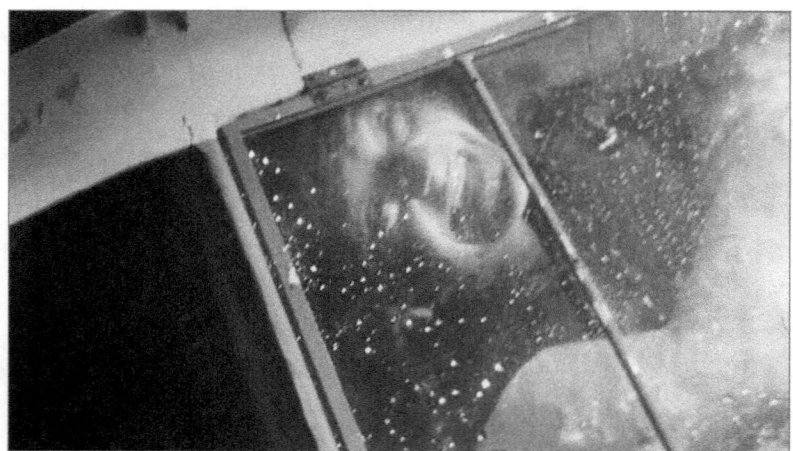

Zeigler's crash; Zeigler trapped in the cockpit.

For the spectacular plane crash and sinking, the company employed the stunt pilot Dean Englehardt with special effects rigged by Marcel Vercomtere. The seaplane, riding the surface of the water, would run over the head of a floating mannequin (doubling for Warren) and then hit the Mexican statue. The impact with the statue would dislodge one of the seaplane's pontoons and cause the plane to crash into the water.

Vercomtere rigged one set of explosives to release the pontoon and a second set to buckle the wings of the plane so it would sink. Penn utilized four camera crews to film the stunt. On one take the plane missed the dummy, tore one of its pontoons, after which the explosives, detonated out of order, severely damaged the plane. The crew had to scramble to reassemble and re-rig the aircraft for another take, putting the company behind schedule.[230]

The botched attempts to film the plane stunt in addition to bad weather meant that the company lost three and a half days of shooting, estimated by observers to cost $80,000.

On November 19 the film's publicist was quoted by the local press: "Everything's very fragile... Everyone's whipped. We've been working on night scenes and sometimes they go on until around three or four in the morning. I've never worked on a picture that's been quite this harried."[231]

. . .

Penn's teenage children Matthew and Molly visited Sanibel for Thanksgiving on November 22, which was also the tenth anniversary of the assassination of President Kennedy. Griffith's mother Tippi Hedren was also on the island and posed for publicity photographs with her daughter.[232] A few

Penn filming the climactic plane crash scene (*The Day of the Director*)

days later Griffith had a minor car accident on Sanibel late at night after filming. She sprained her elbow and suffered some small cuts to her face, but was able to resuming filming on the Monday.[233]

Although there were lighter moments on location, including the wedding of the unit's transportation director – Hackman acted as best man – the shooting was tough on the cast and crew. The brutal fight scene between Harry and Iverson was choreographed in a laborious fashion at Woodring Point one night. Hackman and John Crawford filmed what they could, and the most dangerous moments were performed by stuntmen Glenn Wilder and Chuck Hicks.[234] As scripted, Iverson dies of his fight injuries.

By now, Hackman was worn out. "I've been on location for fifteen out of the last eighteen months," he told the press. "The only thing that could help me now is plasma."[235]

Sharp departed before the shoot had concluded. Although she wasn't aware of it at the time, Warren later realised it was due to a creative disagreement with Penn. Sharp later admitted that by now "the creative threads between me and Arthur had been loosened."[236] That would only get worse in post-production.

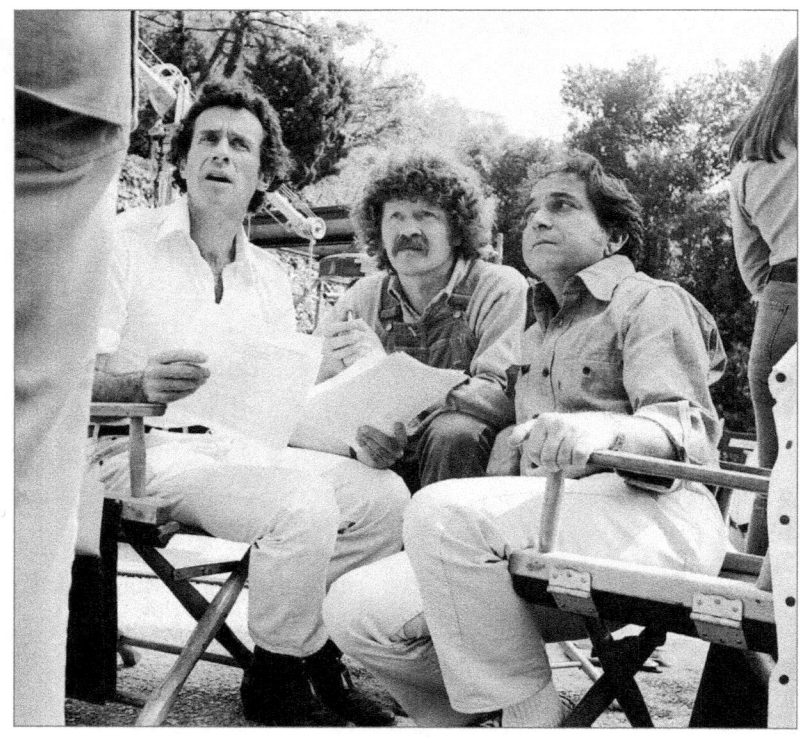

Arthur Penn with Alan Sharp (middle) on the *Night Moves* set

5. Night Moves
(1974)

After the trial of filming, post-production. Penn began to edit his enormous quantity of footage with his regular collaborator Dede Allen and her assistant Steven A. Rotter. The work was based in New York throughout 1974. Sharp visited the editing suite, although he was drifting away from the project and into a new personal crisis.

Penn felt closer to Dede Allen as a collaborator than he ever did to his screenwriters, none of whom he worked with more than once. Allen had joined the team for *Bonnie and Clyde* and became an essential creative partner on all of Penn's films since then. The virtuoso cutting of that film's finale, the spectacularly bloody massacre of the two bandits, was recognised as a milestone in Hollywood history. "We really make the film together by discussing it at length in pre-production and keep communicating throughout the shoot," Penn explained in 1977. Allen would visit Penn's sets during filming "to get an idea of location, characters, and general atmosphere." She had "a liberating influence." With Dede Allen, Penn said, "everything is possible. There are no rules. She's the least dogmatic person I know... whatever the technical or stylistic problems she never considers it hopeless." Penn described the partnership "as close as two collaborators can be."[237]

Assistant editor Steven A. Rotter praised Allen's lack of "fear of making bold choices. No stone was left unturned. Her dedication and her stick-to-it-iveness were legendary... Her eye was always on the story and the performance. Arthur loved to do bold things both in directing and in editing. It was probably a match made in heaven, the two of them."

Penn was not in the editing room throughout the entire process. Rotter remembered:

> *[Arthur] would screen a film, give notes, go away, come back, screen it again, maybe have friends come and see it. But it was mostly through note-taking and discussion... Arthur preferred to go away, stay as fresh as possible, come back, look, and give another set of notes.*[238]

Penn's time-consuming accumulation of coverage for each scene had some consequences for continuity. The actor's movements were not always repeated identically in every take in every camera set-up, resulting in some occasional spatial discontinuities from cut to cut. Penn and Allen were also bold enough to sometimes break the 180-degree rule that intercut camera angles should always remain on one side of an imaginary line to maintain spatial orientation for the audience.

Early on Penn decided the film "needed abrupt, disjointed, almost convulsive editing, something that might suggest a nervous tic."[239] On occasion Penn and Allen juxtaposed thematically related images to leap from scene to scene. For example, one transition cuts from a detail of a black-and-white TV broadcast of an NFL game to Harry kicking a basketball outside Quentin's garage. Another cuts from a shot of Marty Heller angrily shrugging off Harry to a shot of Harry kicking the fridge door back at his house as if in retaliation.

Penn decided to re-record much of the dialogue in a dubbing studio, and not only to make up for the technical deficiencies of live on-set sound recording. Jennifer Warren was a little puzzled by the extent of the post-synchronisation. "Supposedly Warren Beatty got better when he looped things," she remembers. "Maybe [Penn] got hung up on it because Warren was such a good partner for him." Usually Penn sought a stronger reading of the lines, but occasionally the purpose was to revise the dialogue.

Melanie Griffith's teenage voice was so soft that it was necessary to re-record most of her dialogue, as she would have to do for many of her early films. For the diving scene in which Delly discovers Marv Ellman's drowned body, Penn came up with a novel approach. "They had a huge trashcan full of water," Griffith remembered, "and Arthur was dunking my head."

Penn had first noticed Michael Small's music when he went to the movies with Terrence Malick. Small's present speciality was scoring some of the era's best paranoid conspiracy thrillers. In this genre he frequently combined his sensibilities as a jazz pianist with elements of avant-garde classical music including microtonality and dissonance. He was a master of spare, atmospheric orchestration. He had written an eerie score spotlighting vibraphone, piano, and wordless female vocals for Alan J. Pakula's *Klute* (1971).[240] In February 1974 at Paramount Small recorded his score for Pakula's *The Parallax View*: a series of frightening and often dissonant soundscapes that drew on elements of typical patriotic idioms including military anthems and marches.[241]

Night Moves would be recorded in New York.[242] Despite the conspiracy plot of *Night Moves*, Small's approach was a departure from the Pakula films. Penn suggested Latin jazz elements because of the proximity of the Florida Keys to Cuba. For some reason Small drew not upon Afro-Cuban music but Brazilian rhythms. "My whole score has a Latin-Brazilian feel," Small said.[243] Although the instrumentation unmistakeably renders the score a product of its time, the music makes an invaluable contribution to *Night Moves*' distinctive emotional landscape.

Small explained that "I always find my favourite sequence to start a score with and then I work backwards from that point." He began by writing music for a scene of "a boat moving through murky waters off the Keys with strange Florida undergrowth at the water's edge." None of the boating scenes that match this description are scored in the final cut, but Small had found his main theme. "Later I made an interesting discovery – that the theme would work as a full-out samba which plays in a sudden modulation in a new key. The musical shape is circular, and that is where we are at the end of the film with a boat going round and round without a captain, the existential mystery not having been solved. It's a Latin jazz *La Ronde*."[244]

The score, totalling a mere 15 minutes, consists mostly of variations on that main theme, by turns urgent and tender. Small's cue for the title sequence assigns the theme to solo vibraphone over an insistent samba groove with Fender Rhodes comping and dense chords for flutes and brass. The starring vibraphonist was almost certainly Emil Richards, a prolific session percussionist who had played on many of Small's previous soundtracks as well as on scores for Jerry Goldsmith, Don Ellis, Dave Grusin, Lalo Schifrin, and others.[245] A gentle waltz rendition, performed by an oboe, accompanies Harry's brooding after discovering his wife's infidelity and later as Harry comforts Delly after her nightmare. The final credits transform the theme into that "full-out samba." Other aspects of the score are not as successful. One cue accompanying Paula and Harry's drive to meet Delly at Gulf Shores, scored for an ensemble led by acoustic guitar with a laidback rock beat, is so anomalous that it seems flown-in from a different film.

Some recent pop recordings were subbed in as source music. "If Teardrops Were Pennies" (1973) by Porter Wagoner and Dolly Parton appeared in the New Mexico bar scene, "Quimbara" (1974) by Celia Cruz plays on Harry's rental car radio as he drives across the causeway, and "El Día de Suerte" by Hector Lavoe and Willie Colón (1973) is heard in the background at the Islamorada marina as Delly hangs out with the conchs. The brutal fight between Harry and Iverson is accompanied, ironically, by Ray Barretto's "Indestructible" (1973) on the radio.

Alan Sharp saw an early cut of the film in New York. "It was a fine act and I must say I was very well pleased. However, from my point of view, I thought the piece didn't work. I felt that I hadn't done my job completely; I knew areas which had fallen apart."[246] He believed that despite its many strong scenes and Hackman's performance, there were problems with the pacing. "It never ran like a thriller... The film was kind of floundering. It wasn't getting down the road."[247] Penn had not yet shown the film to executives at Warner Bros. and was nervous. "The four million dollars he had spent making the film was starting to look to him like a lot of money," Sharp said.[248]

Penn and Sherman took an early cut to Hollywood to show to a group of industry colleagues. Neither Sharp nor Warren attended, although both heard about this game-changing event. Screenwriter Robert Towne, whose masterful detective screenplay for *Chinatown* had just reached cinemas in the summer of 1974, was there with ready advice. Other accounts place Bob Rafelson, Mike Nichols, Warren Beatty, Jack Nicholson and Terrence Malick at the screening.[249]

It was the moment Sharp lost all influence over the film's final form. Reports are inconsistent, but Sharp would later infer there had been a consensus at the screening that Harry Moseby was not a particularly sympathetic hero. If true, that couldn't have been a surprise to Penn. After all, he had decided during the screenwriting process that Harry should be more jealous, aggressive, and unlikeable than even in Sharp's original conception. As a character, Harry Moseby was intended to dismantle the detective archetype. He is a man disastrously hamstrung by his macho insecurities and his inability to conceive of motives beyond a limited framework of human behaviour. "Moseby transcended sympathy," Sharp said. "It wasn't necessary to be personally sympathetic to his plight if you were concerned about his allegory."[250]

Jennifer Warren now reflects, "Those men [at the screening] were not like Alan, although Alan obviously admired them... They were very macho males who were not seeing it from the female point of view, which Alan did."[251] Sharp concluded that Penn came to accept the advice of his male colleagues and that Penn's subsequent tweaks to the film were designed to try to improve the audience's identification of Moseby as a classic detective hero – a damaging and pointless endeavour, in Sharp's bitter and lasting judgement. It seemed that Penn's Hollywood colleagues had decided the "scene with Paula was somehow integral to that problem" of audience identification with Moseby. Sharp concluded that Penn had come to agree that the monologue "made Paula so strong a character that Moseby's reaction to her afterwards only enhanced the idea that he didn't know what the fuck he was doing."[252] Of course that was what Sharp actually intended.

Penn went back to New York to do further work in the editing suite. Dede Allen said she considered Warren's sex scene monologue "a wonderful scene, just heart-breaking," while Penn remembered, "I looked at it so many times. It was good in, it was good out." He finally decided to remove it from the film. Dede Allen later said she was "very, very upset" by the decision.[253] Warren learned about the cut when she was called in to re-record the dialogue. She remembers, "Alan and I were disturbed by the cut."[254]

But perhaps Penn, now asserting final authority over this collaborative film, felt that this strange and poetic moment played as a self-consciously literary element in an otherwise realistic drama – regardless of how effectively and bravely Warren performed the monologue. After all, Sharp had a history of writing terrible sex scenes. According to Sherman, Robert Towne gave blunt advice: "Take it out or cut it down." Sherman was pragmatic, saying, "Many times the thing that you fall most in love with in a script is the thing you've got to get rid of: kill your babies."[255]

Penn made other editorial tweaks to downplay the emphasis on Moseby's insecurities and to present the detective as a more traditional hero. A consequence of these minor cuts was to strip out the nuances of Harry and Ellen's marital crisis and also to alleviate its hopelessness, something Penn had already attempted by insisting Sharp rewrite the airport scene. "The overall draft was to minimise Paula's character and to maximise the character of the wife," Sharp said. "Moseby was going to get back with his wife when it was all over – this was to become the positive thing in the film."[256] Although no audience member was likely to walk out of the drama with a shred of hope – *Night Moves* ends in utter despair – the final cut is a marginally more conventional detective film than Sharp wanted, even if Harry's crucial final self-assessment survived: "I haven't solved anything," he says, "it all just fell in on top of me."[257]

What might seem to be minor, surgical cuts had major consequences for the film's characters. In the shooting script, Ellen responds to Harry's dismissal of French arthouse cinema ("like watching paint dry") by identifying it as his "Fred Flintstone bit" which, she says, is "one of the phoniest things about" him.[258] While the couple are obviously riffing on their respective exaggerated personas – Ellen the sophisticated antiques dealer, Harry the philistine football player – we later discover that the "Fred Flintstone" line has hit a nerve with insecure Harry. He resents Ellen's disapproval of his "lifestyle." During their argument in the kitchen after the revelation of Ellen's affair, she admits, "I married you because I thought you were somebody special." Harry adds bitterly, "Only I turned out to be Fred Flintstone."[259]

Penn decided to eliminate the recurring "Fred Flintstone" motif entirely. In the final version, Harry's dismissal of the French movie merely inspires Ellen to give him an affectionate, amused kiss. With this change, the audience is invited to interpret Harry as a loveable down-to-earth hero who sees through pretention.

Penn also abbreviated Harry's brief exchange with Charles at the conclusion of that showroom scene. In the shooting script, when Harry mockingly suggests the two men go bowling together, Charles offers a brave and challenging rejoinder: "You seem to get some weird kind of satisfaction from this sort of thing, don't you? I mean, I'm only a faggot for Godsake." Harry shrugs that off with "Sorry, us rednecks are all alike."[260] With that vaguely self-pitying comment, Harry seems to be suggesting that Charles is the bully, another sophisticate who looks down upon him as a Fred Flintstone. But in the final cut Penn ended the scene just before Charles has a chance to deliver his "I'm only a faggot" line. Now Harry gets the last laugh – in fact, the soundtrack continues with Arlene's laughter in the following scene, as if she is laughing at Charles, too. The bowling joke was therefore reshaped to play in Harry's favour – unpretentious Harry again poking fun at a humourless snob. Harry escapes the scene with his swagger intact. The abbreviation also deprives Charles of his only real moment of dignity. Without the line of dialogue Charles never rises above a 1970s homosexual caricature. Harry's macho homophobia, which Sharp had planted in the scene to reflect the man's insecurities, now simply exists. Penn's version pulls Harry back into the tradition of the wise-cracking shamus, Sam Spade mocking Joe Cairo for his perfumed handkerchief, Phillip Marlowe reflecting that "a pansy has no iron in his bones, whatever he looks like."[261]

Later, when Harry is tormented by Ellen's infidelity, he finds fraternal community with the macho stuntmen he meets in New Mexico. Sharp said that "Moseby's affection for them was intended to be one of the things which would prevent him from perceiving what was happening"[262] – their culpability in the smuggling conspiracy and, even worse, Delly's murder. Several scenes Sharp wrote for these characters did not make the film's final cut. Sharp had written a jokey touch football scene to be played on the New Mexico film set between Harry, Joey Zeigler, and Marv Ellman. It was filmed but Penn removed the scene.[263] It survives in Sharp's novelization. Harry, "absurdly cheerful," plays a trick on Ellman and pretends to be Joey's "cousin from La Jolla" rather than a former professional football player. Like Harry, Ziegler is a homophobe and bluntly physical. During the game Ziegler voices the "scattergun opinion that everyone on the opposing side was a faggot." For Harry "suddenly it all seemed very pleasant to be standing holding a composition football, damp with perspiration in the clear New Mexico air."[264]

Later in the novelization, in an additional scene that didn't make the picture (or the shooting script), Harry and Ziegler leave the NFL game and sit in a bar decorated with western iconography, which Harry thinks of as an "enormous masculine domain of threatened power, of eroded supremacy. In years to come places like this would become illegal, like tattoos or wolf whistles, as strident equality prevailed." Zeigler pitches a vacation to Baja California in Mexico. They will "fish some, swim. Get drunk. Maybe get laid. There's always some hippy chick needing the price of something. If you wash them well first, they're good eating."[265] Harry acquiesces to Joey's fantasy of exploitable young girls, even as it uneasily recalls Delly's situation. The plan is all the more sinister considering it is voiced by the psychopath who will shortly murder her.

The final edit ultimately shines a little light into Sharp's abysmal darkness. Tom Iverson was originally to be killed in his fight with Harry, but Paula's dialogue was redubbed so that Iverson is "still breathing." Penn also deleted a number of other scenes, routine cuts for pacing. There had been a weak prelude of Harry adjudicating a trivial neighbourhood fight over a urinating dog[266]; another scene of Harry living in his office while separated from Ellen[267]; and a scene where Moseby returns to listen to the entirety of Delly's answering machine message after her death. Penn decided the latter scene was redundant, as Quentin has already given Harry the same information. He also liked that its removal "breaks your expectations, that you expect him to go back to the tape and get the truth."[268]

Although critical of his script's weaknesses, Sharp was deeply disappointed that, as he saw it, Penn tried to transform the film into something more conventional. In his view Penn lost his nerve.

> *I think he 'lessened' the piece so that its flaws were not so naked. That hurt me a lot. It was the first time I had ever been creatively offended working*

in Hollywood... That decision to cut [the sex scene monologue] offended me. I felt it was really very weak of Arthur. More to the point, it improved the film in no way. [269]

How did the break-down of the collaboration affect Penn? He never publicly criticised Sharp, but their professional relationship was finished. "I think the dissension afterwards was upsetting for Arthur," Warren says. "I don't think Arthur got into many disputes willingly." Warren's disappointment with the loss of her monologue has faded with time: "I don't think it made as much difference as we thought. But at the time, after having been at such a visceral level with this, it was kind of a sucker punch... [The love scene] is a pretty unprotected place and I think that's why it meant so much to Alan at the time – and me... Now I don't think as badly of the cut."

Penn delivered his director's cut to Warner Brothers and they released it without changes.[270] To avoid a conflict with the 20th Century Fox/Warner Bros disaster film released in December 1974, *The Towering Inferno*, a new title had been chosen.[271] The film would go out as *Night Moves*, a noirish pun on the 1922 chess match at Bad Oyenhaussen in which Bruno Moritz just didn't see the obvious solution.

6. The Shark Tank
(1975)

As post-production wound up on *Night Moves*, Sharp's personal life was in turmoil. Having been fascinated by how his fictional Harry Moseby would react to his wife's infidelity, he now found himself facing the situation in his own marriage.

In fact, in late June 1975, as *Night Moves* played across the country, Sharp wrote an extraordinarily indiscrete account of his ongoing crisis in an essay ostensibly about Scottish football. He described himself sitting stoned in a soccer jersey outside his house in Los Angeles, exchanging small talk with his wife's lover before the man "went on into the only too imaginable delights of my bed." Bizarrely candid, Sharp actually published the name of his wife's current lover in print.[272]

Sharp's essay was soul-searching and self-castigating but also full of his typical literary flourishes. He admitted he was "intent on wrestling an encompassing metaphor out of my life, Scottish football and the history of the race."[273] He had learned of Liz's affair the previous summer at the FIFA

World Cup in Frankfurt (while Penn and Allen were working to finish *Night Moves* in New York). He claimed that by then he had finally decided to "settle down" with Liz after years of deceiving her about his many affairs. But when she arrived in Frankfurt between Scotland's games with Brazil and Yugoslavia, Liz admitted she had a lover. Sharp said it thrust him into a state of great anxiety:

> *In the months that followed my discovery that my wife loved somebody else I experienced an overwhelming dread of being nobody, of being an unloved child, an unworthy lover, a 'depart from me for I know thee not-er'. And worst of all I could not let myself heal... so I would enter my wife's bedroom in order to confront the most specific of all proofs of my unworthiness, her joy at another man's body.*[274]

Liz Sharp remembers that her husband "had a nervous breakdown and lost an enormous amount of weight. He went in for psychotherapy." He went to great lengths to persuade Liz not to leave him. "He won over my family, who had always been a bit like, 'What the hell are you doing with your life, Liz?' And they all went with him! 'What are you doing to Alan, leaving him?'"

Then, at the end of that tumultuous 1975, Beryl Bainbridge published a far-from-flattering *roman à clef* called *Sweet William*, based on her tumultuous relationship with Sharp a decade earlier. Bainbridge later said she "didn't exaggerate his character. If anything I toned him down."[275] The novel unwittingly suggests how much of *Night Moves*' dialogue was taken directly from Sharp's own repertoire. Patting the heroine on the back, William tells her that mothers pat their children that way to create "continuity" with the womb: "We were grown under the heart," he says. (Delly tells Harry much the same thing). William writes a TV play called *The Truth is a Lie* (a recurring motif Penn had eliminated from his final cut).[276] Bainbridge adapted the novel into a screenplay that was directed by Claude Whatham in 1980.

With such distractions in his personal life, Sharp drifted far away from *Night Moves*.

. . .

The film's official world premiere had been on Wednesday, March 26, 1975, the closing night of the Filmex '75 film festival at the Plitt Century Plaza in Century City, Los Angeles.[277] But *Night Moves* had already been shown that month at the USA Film Festival in Dallas. Also screening in Dallas, among a crop of new films, was Michael Ritchie's *Smile*, the second of three near-simultaneous films to launch Melanie Griffith's acting career.[278] She had been selected 'Miss Golden Globe' in January.[279]

Warner Bros had little confidence in *Night Moves*' commercial prospects. Departing the Dallas festival with Bob Sherman, Warner Bros sales executive Larry Leshansky projected box office returns of just $2.5 million. For a film that had cost $4 million, it was a disaster. Sherman found the news "heart-breaking."[280]

The film's trailer emphasized the action scenes. The narrator's pitch was vague but did try to sell the film as a character study in addition to a mystery: "He's a private investigator making a living from other people's lives, making a mess of his own… It's a mystery where the suspects are also the victims, where the questions have too many answers,

Two variants of the US release poster

where every clue is a lie... it's a game where every player is a pawn, every move is a wrong one, and the winner loses everything."²⁸¹ The tagline on the original release poster played on the film's existential aspects: "Maybe he would find the girl... Maybe he would find himself."

But Warner Bros put little effort into pushing the film, and Sherman demanded an explanation from studio president Frank Wells. Sherman remembered:

> *There was some beef over the size of the ad they ran in the* New York Times. *The public was starting to get savvy. If you ran a full-page ad in the* New York Times, *the public recognized, at least in New York and LA, that the studio was behind the picture. But they didn't run a full-page ad.*²⁸²

Melanie Griffith, a few months shy of eighteen, participated in a number of widely-syndicated press interviews. Supposedly part of Hollywood's "teen troupe," one focus was on her celebrity background as the daughter of Tippi Hedren.²⁸³ More exploitative stories focused on her romantic life and the brief flashes of nudity in the film. *The Philadelphia Inquirer* gossiped: "Melanie's a sweet 17 but has been kissed... A vision of old-fashioned loveliness, and yet Melanie's lifestyle befits the modern idea of the independent woman's lib advocate, one who would cause Norman Rockwell to drop his paint brush in horror."²⁸⁴ Years later Griffith assessed the experience:

> *I remember going to New York and doing press for the first time ever in my life, never having been exposed to what that was like, and talk shows... I didn't know anything... You're so young and you're thrown into*

a big shark tank. It wasn't Arthur's responsibility, it was the studio's.[285]

Jennifer Warren was also sent on the publicity trail. Deeply invested in the film, she publicly criticised Penn's decision to cut her monologue, although granted that Penn had "all the fears and doubts and second thoughts that are human," adding "if you don't have a few holdouts like Arthur, flawed human being that he is, then art is lost." Warren was also unafraid to criticise Warner Brothers' campaign and their decision to promote *Night Moves* as a mere genre exercise.[286] Now she reflects:

Warner Bros didn't know how to sell it. They had a terrible campaign, that's one of the reasons why it didn't do well... They chose to sell it wrong. They chose to make it look like an action thriller, so everybody that went to see it came out saying, 'Thanks, that wasn't it.' Warners actually changed the campaign halfway through, which was unusual, but by then it was too late... They didn't want to sell it for what it was.[287]

Much had changed in America in the eighteen months since Penn had wrapped the shoot. Nixon had resigned in disgrace on August 9, 1974, and the following spring the Vietnam War ended with the defeat of US forces. 1975's box office hits suggested audiences were mostly seeking escapism rather than confrontation with the national darkness. *Night Moves*, a belatedly-appearing relic, grounded in the sensibilities of the earlier part of the decade, was a hard sell.

"The public wasn't ready for a film that challenged the sacred laws of genre at a time when most films were slavishly following conventions," Penn said. "We were a few years too late." [288]

Warner Bros finally released *Night Moves* in the US on June 11. Susan Clark, no fan of movie premieres, went to see *Night Moves* as a paying audience member at a matinee screening in a Hollywood theatre. "It was about half-full. When it came to the scene where Gene and I were arguing, and I kept saying 'why? why? why?', some man behind me said, 'Oh shut up, you stupid woman!'" She laughs. "I guess that patron was very sympathetic to Gene Hackman's position."

Mainstream reviews for *Night Moves* were decidedly mixed, and gave little indication that it would come to be considered one of the finest films of the era (Robert Altman's sprawling country music epic *Nashville*, which attracted much of the summer's critical attention, was released the same day). Vincent Canby of the *New York Times* wrote that the characters "seem to deserve better than the quality of the narrative given them."[289] Roger Ebert in the *Chicago Sun-Times* called it "one of the best psychological thrillers in a long time" although he qualified that statement with "Art this isn't."[290] Ebert, along with *Time* magazine's Richard Schickel, focused on *Night Moves*' supposed derivation from the popular Lew Archer novels of Ross Macdonald, the source material for Stuart Rosenberg's *The Drowning Pool*, the other private detective film on Warner Bros' release schedule.[291]

The film's complexity and its downbeat ending, the mixed reviews and Warner Bros' half-hearted campaign: these were only some of the challenges facing *Night Moves* on initial release. It had to fight for market space in a film season that seemed almost calculated to trump its various selling points. Two other Gene Hackman films appeared almost simultaneously and sold a lot more tickets – John Frankenheimer's *The French Connection II* and Richard Brooks' western *Bite The Bullet*.

Genre fans were not starved of alternative choices, either. Just two weeks after *Night Moves*, Warners performed something of an act of self-sabotage by releasing *The Drowning Pool*, in several ways a more conventional refraction of the same elements. Paul Newman reprised the role of Macdonald's classic wise-cracking private dick (previously seen in *Harper* in 1966) and ventured to tropical New Orleans. *The Drowning Pool* also co-starred Melanie Griffith as a promiscuous teen and was scored by Michael Small. That same summer an ageing Robert Mitchum appeared in, as he put it, one of "Victor Mature's old farted-up suits" as Phillip Marlowe in Dick Richards' enjoyable period remake of *Farewell, My Lovely*.[292] But neither *The Drowning Pool* nor *Farewell, My Lovely* had any intention of dismantling the genre. Their heroes were virile, knightly, able to solve the mystery. *Night Moves* proved to be the final expression of the short-lived genre revisionism initiated by *The Long Goodbye*.

The biggest release of the summer – and in the history of cinema to date – was Steven Spielberg's *Jaws*, released just a week and a half after *Night Moves*. During its much-prolonged production the previous year, Jennifer Warren had encountered her friend Roy Scheider while vacationing at Martha's Vineyard. "I said "Roy, what are you doing out here?" And he said, "Oh, my God, I'm making this film about a shark. The blessed shark won't work. It's a nightmare. It's a disaster." [293] But Spielberg managed to overcome the obstacles and deliver the movie audiences wanted to see in the summer of 1975.

In these circumstances, *Night Moves* came and went without much notice.

Alan Sharp's novelization of his screenplay was published by Warner Books as a $1.25 paperback original at the time of the film's release. He dedicated it "To Paula, wherever she may be found." The widely-disparaged genre of the novelized screenplay was hardly likely to attract literary attention; it would have been considered a comedown for a celebrated literary novelist of the 1960s (Sharp had also novelized *The Hired Hand* in 1971). But this dark psychological detective novel is probably Sharp's best piece of prose fiction. It was also his final published novel. The *Night Moves* novelization allowed Sharp to restore those parts of the script which had been modified by Penn. In fact, with what he described as "possibly a little writerly chintz", Sharp sent a copy of the book to Penn with a wry and pointed note:

"Do you think there's a movie in this?"[294]

Coda:
Second Prize in a Fight

As *Night Moves* played cinemas in the summer of 1975, Penn was shooting Thomas McGuane's western screenplay *The Missouri Breaks* with Marlon Brando and Jack Nicholson in Montana. Robert Sherman was again producing. Sharp, reeling from his marriage troubles, visited the set.[295] There may have been some limited personal reconciliation with Penn. Meanwhile, Sharp and Robert Sherman were still in business. Earlier in 1975 Sherman had signed a deal with executive Mike Medavoy at United Artists. One of several projects in the deal was an original screenplay Sharp had finished in late 1974 called *Above the Mountain*, a South American adventure set in the 1930s.[296] The picture was announced but never made. Despite widespread recognition of his talent in the industry, Sharp's five produced original screenplays had not resulted in commercially successful films. It is difficult to imagine his bleak sensibility would have found takers in any other era except during the brief flourishing of New Hollywood. That time had passed.

The back-to-back flops of *Night Moves* and *The Missouri Breaks* seriously damaged Arthur Penn's film career and he never regained his momentum. Other directors brave enough to explore the dark side of America – Coppola, Schatzberg, Rafelson – also saw their careers decline. The sentimental reclamation of the American past as a triumphant narrative was in unstoppable motion. The bicentennial year of 1976 was characterised by displays of patriotism, sentimental nostalgia, and escapism. Hollywood production reflected that change in mood.

Jennifer Warren reflects: "People wanted to move away from all that angst as quickly as their little feet could carry them. It was such a gnarly, dramatic time that people wanted to forget it."[297]

For a time Penn developed a film about the massacre at Attica State Prison based on Tom Wicker's *A Time to Die* (1975); it was ultimately made by director Marvin J. Chomsky as the TV miniseries *Attica* (1980). Penn was far more successful on Broadway with *Sly Fox*, Larry Gelbart's 1976 adaptation of *Volpone*. His return to the cinema, *Four Friends* (1981) was an ambitious, engaging, but sometimes luridly melodramatic attempt to come to terms with the social transformation of America since the early 1960s.

Sharp decided to leave the US when Ronald Reagan was elected President in 1980 and moved to a tranquil hideaway in New Zealand.[298] His marriage to Liz was ending. For a long period after *Night Moves* he had found lucrative work as an uncredited script doctor. His onscreen credits were minor, including Sam Peckinpah's final, confusing thriller *The Osterman Weekend* (1983). But the ambition to make his own film was still there. In 1984 Sharp finally directed the *Tepic in the Morning* script under its new name *Little Treasure* with Margot Kidder, Ted Danson, and Burt Lancaster. The production made the news when Lancaster assaulted Kidder during an altercation on set in Mexico. Around the same time Penn reunited with Gene Hackman and Michael Small for a European-set thriller, *Target*. Blatantly commercial in its ambitions, it was a very weak film from such talented collaborators. Neither *Little Treasure* nor *Target* was well-received on release in 1985.

Although Penn would sporadically return to filmmaking and television into the 1990s, his output was far below the standard he'd established in earlier years. Nevertheless, he remained an important theatre director. He died in 2010. Sharp wrote numerous TV movies including another private detective story, *Love and Lies* (directed by Roger Young in 1989), which he later cited among his best work. He did not put *Night Moves* on the list.[299] Late in his career he wrote the excellent Scottish adventure film *Rob Roy* (Michael Caton-Jones, 1995) and *Dean Spanley* (Toa Fraser, 2008). He died in 2013.

Sharp never seemed to make peace with the final form of *Night Moves* and in interviews tended to describe it as something of a failure – both in his writing and in Penn's post-production. For his part, Penn admitted that going back to work hadn't dragged him out of his personal crisis. He was still searching for direction as an artist. In 1976 he described *Night Moves* and *The Missouri Breaks* as "not what I really feel close to... My last two films haven't been very good because I've made too many compromises with Hollywood, something I really need to stop doing. I'm going to devote myself to changing the direction of my life and in turn my films. Not so I can get back to the way I was before my 'crisis,' but so I can be true to my interests and to myself. I'll never again work on something I'm not truly passionate about."[300]

And yet the ultimate dissatisfaction of both key collaborators is now beside the point. *Night Moves* may not have turned out exactly the way Sharp and Penn intended, but it stands as the best film either collaborator made – a bold and compassionate interrogation of American mythology in a time of disillusionment from sea to shining sea.

Appendix:
Film Credits

Directed by Arthur Penn
Written by Alan Sharp
Produced by Robert M. Sherman

CAST
Harry Moseby | Gene Hackman
Ellen | Susan Clark
Paula | Jennifer Warren
Ziegler | Edward Binns
Marty Heller | Harris Yulin
Nick | Kenneth Mars
Arlene Iverson | Janet Ward
Quentin | James Woods
Marv Ellman | Anthony Costello
Tom Iverson | John Crawford
Delly Grastner | Melanie Griffith
Charles | Ben Archibek
Boy | Dennis Dugan
Girl | C.J. Hincks
Stud | Maxwell Gail, Jr.
Ticket Clerks | Susan Barrister, Larry Mitchell

Music Composed and Conducted by Michael Small
Director of Photography | Bruce Surtees
Film Editor | Dede Allen
Production Designer | George Jenkins
Associate Producer | Gene Lasko

Unit Production Manager | Thomas J. Schmidt
Sound Mixer | Jack Solomon
Re-Recording | Richard Vorisek

Assistant Art Director | David Haber
Set Decorator | Ned Parsons

Costume Supervision | Rita Riggs
Costumer | Arnie Lipin
Titles | Wayne Fitzgerald
Assistant to Producer | Bonnie Bruckheimer

Co-editor | Stephen A. Rotter
Assistant Editors | Ronald Roose, Angelo Corrao
Sound Editors | Robert Reitano, Richard Cirincione, Craig McKay

Assistant Director | Jack Roe
Script Supervisor | Marshall Schlom
Camera Operators | Robert C. Thomas, Ozzie Smith, Jim Pergola

Underwater Camera | Jordan Klein
Aerial Coordinator | Dean Englehardt
Location Auditor | Gordon Kee
Casting | Nessa Hyams

Special Effects | Marcel Vercoutere, Joe Day
Gaffer | Chuck Holmes
Key Grip | Bill Simpson
Transportation | Joe Sawyers

Property Master | Barry Bedig
Make-Up | Bob Stein
Hairdressers | Irene Aparicio, Bruce Jossen
2nd Assistant Director | Patrick H. Kehoe

Filmed with Panavision Equipment
Technicolor

A Hiller Productions, Ltd.-Layton Production

Warner Bros, 1975

Notes and References

EPIGRAPH

1   Raymond Chandler, *The Big Sleep* (New York: Vintage, 1992), 156.

PROLOGUE: THE EDGE OF AMERICA

2   Thomas McGuane, *Ninety-Two In The Shade* (New York: Bantam, 1974 [1973]), 1.

3   John Barkham, 'Self-Identification Pervades Sharp's Work', *Fort Lauderdale News*, 16 May 1968, 6H.

4   Bruce Horsfield, '*Night Moves* Revisited: Scriptwriter Alan Sharp Interviewed by Bruce Horsfield, December 1979', *Literature/Film Quarterly* vol. 11 no. 2, 1983, 101.

5   Maureen Bashaw, "Dark Tower' Florida Film 'Whodunit' Was Written With A Brogue', *News-Press* (Fort Meyers, Florida), 13 November 1973, D31.

6   Interview with Alan Sharp by Nat Segaloff, 17 October 2006. Courtesy of Nat Segaloff.

7   Horsfield, '*Night Moves* Revisited', 90.

8   Claire Clouzot 'Interview with Arthur Penn' (1976 interview), translated by Paul Cronin and Remi Guillochon, in Michael Chaiken and Paul Cronin (eds.), *Arthur Penn: Interviews*. (Jackson: University Press of Mississippi, 2008), 102-103.

CHAPTER 1: THE BALTIMORE BENCH

9   'Gene Hackman', *Inside the Actors Studio* (Bravo TV). Air date: 14 October 2001.

10 Tom Shields, 'Chasing Hemingway on a Galloping Horse', *Glasgow Herald Weekender*, 5 September 1992, 12.

11 Michel Delain, 'The First Cheyenne Film Director' (1971 interview) in Chaiken and Cronin, *Arthur Penn: Interviews*, 76.

12 Richard Schickel, 'Arthur Penn' (1990 Interview) in Chaiken and Cronin, *Arthur Penn: Interviews*, 188.

13 Tag Gallagher, 'Night Moves' (Interview with Arthur Penn), *Sight and Sound*, 44.2, Spring 1975, 89.

14 These biographical details are taken from Nat Segaloff, *Arthur Penn: American Director* (Lexington: University Press of Kentucky, 2011).

15 Telephone interview with Robert M. Sherman by Nat Segaloff, 12 June 2008.

Courtesy of Nat Segaloff.

16 Richard Combs, 'Arthur Penn' (1981 seminar at the National Film Theatre, London) in Chaiken and Cronin, *Arthur Penn: Interviews*, 136.

17 Clouzot, 'Interview with Arthur Penn', 108.

18 Robert Hughes, 'Arthur Penn, 1922-:Themes and Variations' (1970 interview) in Chaiken and Cronin, *Arthur Penn: Interviews*, 53.

19 Vidal was displeased by Leslie Stevens' adaptation of his teleplay, and later wrote his own feature-length television movie, *Gore Vidal's Billy the Kid* (1989), starring Val Kilmer. See Gore Vidal, *Palimpsest* (New York: Random House, 1995).

20 Arthur Penn, 'Arthur Penn at Dartmouth College' (20 May 1968 speech) in Chaiken and Cronin, *Arthur Penn: Interviews*, 27-28.

21 Alan Sharp, 'A Dream of Perfection' in Ian Archer & Trevor Royle, *We'll Support You Ever More: The Impertinent Saga of Scottish Fitba* (Edinburgh: Edinburgh Mainstream Publishing, 2000 [1976]), 221, 222.

22 W. Gordon Smith, 'Two Thirds of Alan Sharp', *Scottish International*, January 1972, 24.

23 Alan Sharp interview in the documentary *The Odd Man* (Charles Gormley, 1978).

24 Author's telephone interview with Liz Sharp, 9 October 2017. All subsequent quotations of Liz Sharp are from this interview.

25 Barkham, 'Self-Identification Pervades Sharp's Work', 6H.

26 Smith, 'Two Thirds of Alan Sharp', 21.

27 Alan Sharp quoted in Brendan King, *Beryl Bainbridge: Love by All Sorts of Means* (London: Bloomsbury, 2016), 251.

28 Bill Campbell, 'A Green Tree in Hollywood', *The Scotsman*, 28 July 1979.

29 See King, *Beryl Bainbridge*.

30 Tom Shields, 'Chasing Hemingway on a Galloping Horse', *Glasgow Herald Weekender*, 5 September 1992, 12-13; interview with Liz Sharp.

31 Horsfield, '*Night Moves* Revisited', 104.

32 Alan Sharp, *A Green Tree in Gedde* (Glasgow: Richard Drew, 1985 [1965]), 350.

33 King, *Beryl Bainbridge*, 266.

34 Dick Schaap, 'Catering to the Trade', *New York* magazine, 13 May 1968, 56; Walker & Co. advertisement in *Publisher's Weekly*, vol. 193, (1968), 177.

35 Barkham, 'Self-Identification Pervades Sharp's Work', 6H.

36 Barkham, 'Self-Identification Pervades Sharp's Work', 6H.

37 Smith, 'Two Thirds of Alan Sharp', 25.

38 Alan Sharp, 'In the Shade of New Mexico', *West Magazine (Los Angeles Times)*, 26 May 1968, 22.

39 Robert F. Kennedy Indianapolis speech, 4 April 1968, quoted at http://www.americanrhetoric.com/speeches/rfkonmlkdeath.html [Accessed 17 Nov 2017].

40 Mark Harris, *Scenes from a Revolution: The Birth of the New Hollywood* (Edinburgh: Canongate, 2008), 407.
41 Horsfield, '*Night Moves* Revisited', 92.
42 Sharp, 'In the Shade of New Mexico,' 22, 24, 25.
43 Alan Sharp, 'California from Alpha to Omega', *West Magazine* (*Los Angeles Times*), 28 July 1968, 23.
44 Alan Sharp, 'Colorado, Utah, Montana', *West Magazine* (*Los Angeles Times*), 4 May 1969, 42.
45 Penn, 'Arthur Penn at Dartmouth College', 28.
46 Damien Love, 'The Miracle Worker: An Interview with Arthur Penn', *Bright Lights Film Journal*, 31 July 2009. http://brightlightsfilm.com/the-miracle-worker-an-interview-with-arthur-penn/amp/ [Accessed 17 Nov 2017].
47 Delain, 'The First Cheyenne Film Director', 77.
48 Gerard Langlois, '*Candide* in the Wild West' (1971 interview), translated by Paul Cronin and Remi Guillochon, in Chaiken and Cronin, *Arthur Penn: Interviews*, 80.
49 King, *Beryl Bainbridge*, 308.
50 Anon, 'The Novel in the next six months,' *The Guardian*, 10 September 1970, 10.
51 Campbell, 'A Green Tree in Hollywood'.
52 Smith, 'Two Thirds of Alan Sharp', 24.
53 Alan Sharp, 'White Man Unforks Tongue for *Ulzana*', *Los Angeles Times*, 13 May 1972, 20.
54 Horsfield, '*Night Moves* Revisited', 88.
55 Sharp quoted in *The Odd Man*.
56 Anon, 'Blaustein Adds *No Tears* Film', *Abilene Reporter-News*, 20 April 1969, 8B.
57 PHS, 'The *Times* diary', *The Times*, 26 Jan 1970, 8.
58 Alan Sharp interview (1993) in the documentary *Sam Peckinpah, Man of Iron: The Director's Cut* (Paul Joyce, 2017), a special feature on Blu-ray disc of *Bring Me The Head of Alfredo Garcia* (UK: Arrow Films, 2017 [1974]).
59 Anon, 'Fonda Tells Reason For Film Choice', *Victoria Advocate*, 7 November 1971, 27.
60 Susan Compo, *Warren Oates: A Wild Life* (Lexington: University Press of Kentucky, 2009), 209.
61 Smith, 'Two Thirds of Alan Sharp', 22; author interview with Liz Sharp.
62 Horsfield, '*Night Moves* Revisited', 88.
63 Brian Hoyle, *The Cinema of John Boorman* (Lanham: Scarecrow Press, 2012), 60.
64 Anon, 'Actor George C. Scott Doesn't Want To Get In A Rut', *Denton Record Chronicle*, 15 July 1971, 9A.
65 Smith, 'Two Thirds of Alan Sharp', 25.

66 Kate Buford, *Burt Lancaster: An American Life* (London: Aurum, 2008 [2000]), 313.

67 Clarus Backes, 'And now, the award for best actor in a near-disaster filmed by Hollywood on foreign soil', *Chicago Tribune Magazine*, 11 April 1971, 18-28.

68 Joyce Haber, 'Fleischer Just Not Much of a Talker', *Los Angeles Times Calendar*, 1 Aug 1971, 15.

69 Campbell, 'A Green Tree in Hollywood'.

70 Clouzot, 'Interview with Arthur Penn', 102.

71 Jean-Pierre Coursodon, 'Arthur Penn' (1977 interview), translated by Paul Cronin and Remi Guillochon, in Chaiken and Cronin, *Arthur Penn: Interviews*, 111.

72 Author's telephone interview with Matthew Penn, 23 October 2017. All subsequent quotations of Matthew Penn are from this interview.

73 Richard Schickel, 'Arthur Penn' (1990 interview), in Chaiken and Cronin, *Arthur Penn: Interviews*, 186.

74 Michel Ciment, 'Interview with Arthur Penn (1982), translated by Paul Cronin and Remi Guillochon, in Chaiken and Cronin, *Arthur Penn: Interviews*, 155.

75 Richard Schickel, 'Arthur Penn', 186.

76 Coursodon, 'Arthur Penn', 112.

77 Love, 'The Miracle Worker'.

78 Interview with Alan Sharp by Nat Segaloff, 17 October 2006.

79 Sharp, 'In the Shade of New Mexico', 24.

80 See Mitchell Lifton, 'Billy Two Hats some scenes during production' at http://mitchell-lifton.com/Billy-two-hats.html [Accessed 17 Nov 2017].

81 Schickel, 'Arthur Penn', 186.

CHAPTER 2: AN END OF WISHING

82 *Catalog of Copyright Entries: Third series. Volume 26, Parts 3-4, Number 1: Dramas and Works Prepared for Oral Delivery, January-June 1972* (Washington: Library of Congress, 1972), 64; at https://hdl.handle.net/2027/pst.000059864530 [Accessed 23 Nov 2017].

83 Alan Sharp, 'Mexico: Reflections in a Rear-View Mirror', *West Magazine (Los Angeles Times)*, 20 December 1970, 32-33.

84 Smith, 'Two Thirds of Alan Sharp', 22, 26.

85 In the interim director Monte Hellman developed the project, and considered casting Warren Oates and Candy Clark. Earlier Hellman had been considered as the director of *Billy Two Hats*. See Brad Stevens, *Monte Hellman: His Life and Films* (Jefferson, NC: McFarland, 2003), 119.

86 Horsfield, '*Night Moves* Revisited', 101.

87 Buford, *Burt Lancaster*, 312; Jane Bussey, '"Rainmaker" has haymaker for Lois Lane', *United Press International*, 29 February 1984, at https://www.upi.com/Archives/1984/02/29/Rainmaker-has-haymaker-for-Lois-Lane/2918446878800/ [Accessed 5 Dec 2017].

88 Smith, 'Two Thirds of Alan Sharp', 26.
89 Interview with Alan Sharp by Nat Segaloff, 17 October 2006.
90 Email from Dan Sharp to author, 25 September 2017.
91 In the novelization, Paula quips "Childe Harold to Dark Tower came" when Harry first meets Delly. Harry, surprisingly, knows the poem well enough to correct her quotation. Alan Sharp, *Night Moves* (Novelization), (London: Corgi, 1975), 67.
92 *Film Bulletin*, Volumes 43-44, (Wax Publications, 1974), liii; Telephone interview with Robert M. Sherman by Nat Segaloff, 12 June 2008.
93 See Janet L. Meyer, *Sydney Pollack: A Critical Filmography* (Jefferson, N.C.: McFarland, 2008 [1998]), 23-24.
94 Segaloff, *Arthur Penn: American Director*, 203.
95 Author's telephone interview with Bonnie Bruckheimer, 31 August 2017.
96 Alan Sharp, *Night Moves (The Dark Tower) Production #135038* (Shooting Script dated 17 September 1973), 19. Published at the *Cinephilia & Beyond* website, https://cinephiliabeyond.org/arthur-penns-night-moves-demands-deserves-multiple-viewings-every-single-one-equally-rewarding/ [Accessed 13 Dec 2017]; In *Out of the Past*, Jane Greer questions Robert Mitchum about roulette: "Is there any way to win?" He answers: "There's a way to lose more slowly." Alan Sharp, typically, found a way to make the classic comment more hopeless.
97 See Bosley Crowther, "The Career and the Cult," in *Playboy* (June, 1966); See Stefan Kanfer, *Tough Without A Gun: The Life and Extraordinary Afterlife of Humphrey Bogart* (New York: Vintage, 2011).
98 Al Clark, *Raymond Chandler in Hollywood*, (London: Proteus Press, 1982), 124-127.
99 Billy Danreuther, whom Paula remembers as the first person to touch her breast, is also the name of Bogart's character in John Huston's *Beat the Devil* (1954).
100 Sharp, *Night Moves (The Dark Tower)* (Shooting Script), 10.
101 Sharp, *Night Moves (The Dark Tower)* (Shooting Script), 6.
102 Campbell, 'A Green Tree in Hollywood'.
103 Brian Pendreigh, 'Sharp Shooter' (undated interview with Alan Sharp), *Inside Out Film*, at http://www.iofilm.co.uk/feats/interviews/a/alan_sharp.shtml [Accessed 23 Nov 2017].
104 Campbell, 'A Green Tree in Hollywood'.
105 Horsfield, '*Night Moves* Revisited', 88-89.
106 Horsfield, '*Night Moves* Revisited', 98.
107 Horsfield, '*Night Moves* Revisited', 90.
108 Horsfield, '*Night Moves* Revisited', 88.
109 Interview with Alan Sharp by Nat Segaloff, 17 October 2006.
110 Author's telephone interview with Bonnie Bruckheimer, 31 August 2017.
111 Telephone interview with Robert M. Sherman by Nat Segaloff, 12 June 2008.

112 Horsfield, '*Night Moves* Revisited', 89.
113 Anon, 'Arthur Penn to direct "Dark Tower"', *Greeley Daily Tribune*, 29 May 1973, 23.
114 Interview with Alan Sharp by Nat Segaloff, 17 October 2006.
115 Horsfield, '*Night Moves* Revisited', 91.
116 Coursodon, 'Arthur Penn', 113.
117 Clouzot, 'Interview with Arthur Penn', 103.
118 Raymond Chandler, 'The Simple Art of Murder', in *The Art of the Mystery Story*, Howard Haycraft (ed.) (New York: Carroll, 1985), 237.
119 Gallagher, 'Night Moves', 88.
120 Horsfield, '*Night Moves* Revisited', 94.
121 Horsfield, '*Night Moves* Revisited', 94.
122 Sharp, *Night Moves (The Dark Tower)* (Shooting Script), 64.
123 Raymond Chandler, The Big Sleep (New York: Vintage, 1992), 156.
124 Sharp, *Night Moves* (Novelization), 20.
125 Sharp, *Night Moves* (Novelization), 25.
126 Sharp, *Night Moves* (Novelization), 40.
127 Sharp, *Night Moves* (Novelization), 88.
128 Sharp, *Night Moves* (Novelization), 10.
129 Sharp, *Night Moves* (Novelization), 28-29.
130 The director Richard Rush has suggested that in developing *Night Moves*, Penn drew on aspects of Paul Brodeur's 1970 novel *The Stuntman*, which Penn had supposedly once considered directing; Rush was the project's ultimate director in 1980. See Rush's comments in *The Sinister Saga of Making 'The Stunt Man'* (Richard Rush, 2000).
131 Horsfield, '*Night Moves* Revisited', 98.
132 Horsfield, '*Night Moves* Revisited', 100.
133 Dashiell Hammett, 'Fly Paper' in *The Big Knockover* (New York: Vintage, 1972), 38.
134 Chandler, *The Big Sleep*, 159.
135 Horsfield, '*Night Moves* Revisited', 104.
136 Sharp, *Night Moves (The Dark Tower)* (Shooting Script), 50, 21.
137 Sharp, *Night Moves (The Dark Tower)* (Shooting Script), 42.
138 Sharp, *Night Moves (The Dark Tower)* (Shooting Script), 10.
139 Sharp, *Night Moves (The Dark Tower)* (Shooting Script), 113.
140 Sharp, *Night Moves* (Novelization), 77.
141 Sharp, *Night Moves (The Dark Tower)* (Shooting Script), 114.
142 Sharp, *Night Moves (The Dark Tower)* (Shooting Script), 70.
143 Interview with Alan Sharp by Nat Segaloff, 17 October 2006.

144 Sharp, *Night Moves (The Dark Tower)* (Shooting Script), 81.
145 Coursodon, 'Arthur Penn', 114.
146 Horsfield, '*Night Moves* Revisited', 95.
147 Gallagher, 'Night Moves', 89.
148 A minor scandal erupted in 1987, just before Huston's death, when several life-sized statues formerly in his possession were revealed to be fakes. The press had fun with *The Maltese Falcon* echoes. See Nat Moss, 'The Jockey and the Showman', *Vanity Fair*, 15 January 2009. https://www.vanityfair.com/news/2009/01/pearson200901 [Accessed 18 Dec 2017].
149 UNESCO, *Convention Concerning the Protection of the World Cultural and Natural Heritage* (1972), http://whc.unesco.org/archive/convention-en.pdf [Accessed 18 Dec 2017].
150 Horsfield, '*Night Moves* Revisited', 98.
151 Gallagher, 'Night Moves', 88.
152 Interview with Alan Sharp by Nat Segaloff, 17 October 2006.
153 Sharp, *Night Moves (The Dark Tower)* (Shooting Script), 55.
154 Sharp, *Night Moves (The Dark Tower)* (Shooting Script), 80.
155 Sharp, *Night Moves* (Novelization), 99-100.

CHAPTER 3: THE FIRST SIX FEET
156 Segaloff, *Arthur Penn: American Director*, 207.
157 Sharp, *Night Moves (The Dark Tower)* (Shooting Script), 95-95A. Jonathan Kirshner suggests the specifics of that moment of discovery and retreat from reconciliation with the father were borrowed from the life of director François Truffaut. See Jonathan Kirshner, *Hollywood's Last Golden Age: Politics, Society, and the Seventies Film in America* (Ithaca and London: Cornell University Press, 2012), 184.
158 'Gene Hackman', *Inside the Actors Studio.*
159 'Gene Hackman', *Inside the Actors Studio.*
160 Schickel, 'Arthur Penn', 187.
161 Interview with Alan Sharp by Nat Segaloff, Los Angeles, 17 October 2006.
162 Horsfield, '*Night Moves* Revisited', 91.
163 Bob Keaton, 'Sloe-Eyed Jennifer: Outspoken Stage Star Pleads for Subsidies for the Arts', *Fort Lauderdale News*, 22 June 1975, 6E.
164 Author's Skype interview with Jennifer Warren, 21 October 2016; Clouzot, 'Interview with Arthur Penn', 108.
165 Interview with Alan Sharp by Nat Segaloff, Los Angeles, 17 October 2006; Char Warman, 'Stage Actress Begins Film Career With Style' (Gail Strickland interview), *The Cincinnati Enquirer*, 14 July 1975, 29.
166 Author's Skype interview with Jennifer Warren, 21 October 2016.
167 Author's telephone interview with Susan Clark, 14 March 2018. All quoted comments by Susan Clark are from this interview.

168 Hedren and Griffith would later perform with the lions in a notoriously dangerous film shoot for Marshall's *Roar!* (1981).
169 Anon, 'Tippi Hedren's Daughter Hits Film Industry', *Colorado Springs Gazette*, 13 October 1973, 32-D.
170 Segaloff, *Arthur Penn: American Director*, 205.
171 Author's Skype interview with Jennifer Warren, 21 October 2016.
172 Author's Skype interview with Jennifer Warren, 21 October 2016.
173 Keaton, 'Sloe-Eyed Jennifer', 6E.
174 Author's Skype interview with Jennifer Warren, 21 October 2016.
175 All of the replacement pages are dated and therefore Sharp's revisions can be tracked chronologically.
176 Horsfield, '*Night Moves* Revisited', 91.

CHAPTER 4: THE DARK TOWER

177 Gallagher, 'Night Moves', 89.
178 Coursodon, 'Arthur Penn', 129.
179 Gallagher, 'Night Moves', 89.
180 Telephone interview with Robert M. Sherman by Nat Segaloff, 12 June 2008.
181 Horsfield, '*Night Moves* Revisited', 97.
182 Dennis McLennan, 'Bruce Surtees dies at 74; cinematographer worked with Eastwood and Fosse', *Los Angeles Times*, 2 March 2012. http://articles.latimes.com/2012/mar/02/local/la-me-bruce-surtees-20120301 [Accessed 13 Dec 2017].
183 Love, 'The Miracle Worker'.
184 A production still shows Penn and Hackman filming in the empty stadium.
185 Sharp, *Night Moves (The Dark Tower)* (Shooting Script), 9.
186 Sharp, *Night Moves (The Dark Tower)* (Shooting Script), 13.
187 Sharp, *Night Moves (The Dark Tower)* (Shooting Script), 14.
188 Sharp, *Night Moves (The Dark Tower)* (Shooting Script), 15.
189 Horsfield, '*Night Moves* Revisited', 93.
190 Interview with Alan Sharp by Nat Segaloff, 17 October 2006.
191 Horsfield, '*Night Moves* Revisited', 93.
192 Sharp, *Night Moves (The Dark Tower)* (Shooting Script), 51/52.
193 Telephone interview with Robert M. Sherman by Nat Segaloff, 12 June 2008.
194 Sharp, *Night Moves* (Novelization), 134.
195 Telephone interview with Robert M. Sherman by Nat Segaloff, 12 June 2008.
196 Horsfield, '*Night Moves* Revisited', 93.
197 Horsfield, '*Night Moves* Revisited', 98-99.
198 McGuane, *Ninety-Two In The Shade*, 30.

199 Jerry Schwartz, 'Trials and Tribulations on Florida's Sanibel Island', *Philadelphia Inquirer*, 20 December 1973, 4-H.
200 Interview with Alan Sharp by Nat Segaloff, 17 October 2006.
201 Maureen Bashaw, '*Dark Tower* Stars Filming On Sanibel', *Fort Myers News-Press*, 30 October 1973, 1.
202 Maureen Bashaw, 'Stand-In Glory', *Fort Myers News-Press*, 2 December 1973, 16-D.
203 Susan Taylor, 'Movie Cook Moves', *Fort Myers News-Press*, 22 November 1973, 1-D.
204 Author's telephone interview with Liz Sharp, 9 October 2017.
205 Interview with Alan Sharp by Nat Segaloff, 17 October 2006.
206 Interview with Melanie Griffith by Nat Segaloff, 18 May 2006. Courtesy of Nat Segaloff.
207 Bashaw, ''Dark Tower' Stars Filming On Sanibel'.
208 Susan Taylor, 'Sanibel Causeway Hits Big Time', *Fort Myers News-Press*, 1 November 1973, 2-B.
209 Maureen Bashaw, '30 Feet From Hackman, And... Well... Ah... Blank', *Fort Myers News-Press,* 2 November 1973, 1-D.
210 Schwartz, 'Trials and Tribulations on Florida's Sanibel Island'.
211 Author's Skype interview with Jennifer Warren, 21 October 2016.
212 Author's Skype interview with Jennifer Warren, 21 October 2016.
213 Sharp, *Night Moves (The Dark Tower)* (Shooting Script), 48. Sharp would insert this signature line into his adapted screenplay for Sam Peckinpah's *The Osterman Weekend* (1983). See Bernard Frank Dukore, *Sam Peckinpah's Feature Films* (Urbana and Chicago, University of Illinois Press, 1999), 195. Sharp would also use a variation of the line in his screenplay for *Rob Roy* (1995).
214 Maureen Bashaw, 'A Content Gene Hackman Laments Theatre Apathy', *Fort Myers News-Press*, 6 November 1973, 1-D.
215 Bashaw, ''Dark Tower' Florida Film 'Whodunit' Was Written With A Brogue'.
216 The promotional film, directed by Ronald Saland, would be called *Day of the Director*, a jokey reference to Mike Nichol's new film *Day of the Dolphin*, released in December.
217 Author's Skype interview with Jennifer Warren, 21 October 2016.
218 Gallagher, 'Night Moves', 89.
219 'Gene Hackman', *Inside the Actors Studio*.
220 Author's Skype interview with Jennifer Warren, 21 October 2016.
221 Horsfield, '*Night Moves* Revisited', 91.
222 Interview with Melanie Griffith by Nat Segaloff, 18 May 2006.
223 Maureen Bashaw, 'Patience, Frenzy, Danger: On The Set', *Fort Myers News-Press*, 3 December 1973, 6-B.
224 Schwartz, 'Trials and Tribulations on Florida's Sanibel Island'.

225 Interview with Alan Sharp by Nat Segaloff, 17 October 2006.
226 Schwartz, 'Trials and Tribulations on Florida's Sanibel Island'.
227 Horsfield, '*Night Moves* Revisited', 93.
228 Horsfield, '*Night Moves* Revisited', 99; Anon, 'The Scimitar Accident', *Flight*, 12 December 1959, 904.
229 Author's Skype interview with Jennifer Warren, 21 October 2016.
230 Schwartz, 'Trials and Tribulations on Florida's Sanibel Island'.
231 Maureen Bashaw, 'Fragile Situation at Movie', *Fort Myers News-Press*, 19 November 1973, 6-B.
232 Author's telephone interview with Matthew Penn, 23 October 2017.
233 Steve Dougherty, 'When 'Night Moves' was 'Dark Towers'' [sic], *Fort Myers News-Press*, 29 August 1975, D-1.
234 Bashaw, 'Patience, Frenzy, Danger: On The Set'.
235 Schwartz, 'Trials and Tribulations on Florida's Sanibel Island'.
236 Interview with Alan Sharp by Nat Segaloff, 17 October 2006.

CHAPTER 5: NIGHT MOVES

237 Coursodon, 'Arthur Penn', 128-129.
238 Stephen A. Rotter interview by *Movie Geeks United!* podcast 11 April 2013 at https://www.youtube.com/watch?v=tdwUO-ZnJYw [Accessed 20 Dec 2017].
239 Coursodon, 'Arthur Penn', 115.
240 See Helen Hanson, 'Paranoia and Nostalgia: Sonic Motifs and Songs in Neo-Noir' in Mark, Kathrina Glitre, & Greg Tuck (eds), *Neo-Noir* (New York: Wallflower/Columbia University Press, 2009), 44-60.
241 See Scott Bettencourt & Alexander Kaplan, 'The Parallax View' (CD Liner notes) at https://www.filmscoremonthly.com/notes/parallax_view.html [Accessed 20 Dec 2017].
242 Email to author from Andie Childs, American Federation of Musicians. 25 July 2017.
243 Matthais Büdinger, 'Michael Small on *Mountains of the Moon*', *Soundtrack*, Vol. 9, No. 35, 1990, reprinted at http://www.runmovies.eu/michael-small-on-mountains-of-the-moon/ [Accessed 20 Dec 2017].
244 Rudy Koppl, 'Michael Small: Scoring the Director's Vision', *Music from the Movies*, Vol. 21, Autumn 1998, 49.
245 Jon Opstad, 'A Conversation with Emil Richards' at http://www.jonopstad.com/blog/index.php/2015/06/25/a-conversation-with-emil-richards-3/ [Accessed 20 Dec 2017].
246 Horsfield, '*Night Moves* Revisited', 96.
247 Interview with Alan Sharp by Nat Segaloff, 17 October 2006.
248 Horsfield, '*Night Moves* Revisited', 97.
249 Sherman and Warren both cited Towne's presence. Jennifer Warren said the attendees also included directors Mike Nichols and Bob Rafelson (George An-

derson, 'Jennifer Warren Does It Honestly', *Pittsburgh Post Gazette* 13 June 1975, 25); Sharp recalled hearing that Rafelson and Terrence Malick, as well as Warren Beatty and Jack Nicholson had been there (Horsfield, '*Night Moves* Revisited', 96).
250 Horsfield, '*Night Moves* Revisited', 96.
251 Author's Skype interview with Jennifer Warren, 21 October 2016.
252 Horsfield, '*Night Moves* Revisited', 96-97.
253 Kirchner, *Hollywood's Last Golden Age*, 186-187; see also Anderson, 'Jennifer Warren Does It Honestly', 25.
254 Author's Skype interview with Jennifer Warren, 21 October 2016.
255 Telephone interview with Robert M. Sherman by Nat Segaloff, 12 June 2008.
256 Horsfield, '*Night Moves* Revisited', 97.
257 Sharp, *Night Moves (The Dark Tower)* (Shooting Script), 116.
258 Sharp, *Night Moves (The Dark Tower)* (Shooting Script), 8-8A.
259 Sharp, *Night Moves (The Dark Tower)* (Shooting Script), 28.
260 Sharp, *Night Moves (The Dark Tower)* (Shooting Script), 9.
261 Chandler, *The Big Sleep*, 100.
262 Horsfield, '*Night Moves* Revisited', 98.
263 A production still depicting this scene exists and was used to illustrate a lobby card on release.
264 Sharp, *Night Moves* (Novelization), 47-49.
265 Sharp, *Night Moves* (Novelization), 116.
266 Sharp, *Night Moves (The Dark Tower)* (Shooting Script), 1-5; Sharp acknowledged the scene was filmed (see Interview with Alan Sharp by Nat Segaloff, 17 October 2006.)
267 Sharp, *Night Moves (The Dark Tower)* (Shooting Script), 91A-92; A production still depicting this scene exists and was used to illustrate a lobby card on release.
268 Gallagher, 'Night Moves', 88.
269 Horsfield, '*Night Moves* Revisited', 96-97.
270 Gallagher, 'Night Moves', 89.
271 Telephone interview with Robert M. Sherman by Nat Segaloff, 12 June 2008.

CHAPTER 6: THE SHARK TANK
272 Alan Sharp, 'A Dream of Perfection' in Ian Archer & Trevor Royle (eds), *We'll Support You Ever More: The Impertinent Saga of Scottish Fitba* (Edinburgh: Mainstream Publishing, 2000 [1976]), 209-210.
273 Sharp, 'A Dream of Perfection', 219.
274 Sharp, 'A Dream of Perfection', 225-226.
275 Anon, "Beryl Bainbridge' (obituary), *The Telegraph*, 2 July 2010, at http://www.telegraph.co.uk/news/obituaries/culture-obituaries/film-obituar-

ies/7868008/Dame-Beryl-Bainbridge.html [Accessed 22 Dec 2017].
276 Beryl Bainbridge, *Sweet William* (Glasgow: Fontana, 1976 [1975]), 43, 55.
277 Filmex '75 advertisement in *The Los Angeles Times Calendar*, 16 March 1975, 4.
278 Anon, 'Film Festival', *Grand Prairie Daily News*, 7 March 1975, 9.
279 TV Guide in *The Buffalo Grove Herald*, 24 January 1975, 8.
280 Telephone interview with Robert M. Sherman by Nat Segaloff, 12 June 2008.
281 *Night Moves* theatrical trailer (1975).
282 Telephone interview with Robert M. Sherman by Nat Segaloff, 12 June 2008.
283 Tim White, 'Tippi Hedren's Daughter Melanie Joins Hollywood's "Teen Troupe"', *Florence Morning News,* 24 Aug 1975, 6-C.
284 Bob Lardine, 'Melanie's a Sweet 17, But Has Been Kissed', *The Philadelphia Inquirer*, 20 June 1975, 8-B. See also Earl Wilson, 'Her Nudity Scenes Are "No Big Deal"', *Asheville Citizen-Times*, 30 April 1975, 12.
285 Interview with Melanie Griffith by Nat Segaloff, 18 May 2006.
286 Tom McElfresh, 'Studio Merchandising Can Be Unkindest Cut of All', *The Cincinnati Enquirer*, 29 June 1975, 2-F; See also Anderson, 'Jennifer Warren Does It Honestly', 25.
287 Author's Skype interview with Jennifer Warren, 21 October 2016.
288 Clouzot, 'Interview with Arthur Penn', 103.
289 Vincent Canby, 'Night Moves', *New York Times*, 12 June 1975, reprinted at http://www.nytimes.com/movie/review?res=EE05E7DF173EB82CA1494CC6B679998C6896. [Accessed 22 Dec 2017].
290 Roger Ebert, 'Night Moves', *Chicago Sun-Times*, 11 June 1975 reprinted at https://www.rogerebert.com/reviews/night-moves-1975 [Accessed 22 Dec 2017]. Ebert would later include the film in his category of 'Great Movies'.
291 Richard Schickel, 'Cinema: Eye of Fashion', *Time*, 21 July 1975, reprinted at http://content.time.com/time/magazine/article/0,9171,913302,00.html [Accessed 23 Dec 2017].
292 Lee Server, *Robert Mitchum: 'Baby, I Don't Care'* (London: Faber, 2001 [2001]), 560.
293 Author's Skype interview with Jennifer Warren, 21 October 2016.
294 Interview with Alan Sharp by Nat Segaloff, 17 October 2006.

CODA: SECOND PRIZE IN A FIGHT
295 Telephone interview with Robert M. Sherman by Nat Segaloff, 12 June 2008.
296 Anon, 'Producer Signs Picture Deal', *Pittsburgh Post-Gazette*, 12 May 1975, 13; *Catalog of Copyright Entries: Third series. Volume 28, Parts 3-4, Number 1: Dramas and Works Prepared for Oral Delivery, January-June 1974* (Washington: Library of Congress, 1974), 227; at https://babel.hathitrust.org/cgi/pt?q1=sharp%2C%20alan;id=mdp.39015085477399;view=1up;seq=301;num=277;start=1;sz=10;page=search [Accessed 22 Dec 2017].
297 Author's Skype interview with Jennifer Warren, 21 October 2016.

298 Shields, 'Chasing Hemingway on a Galloping Horse', 13.
299 Anon, 'Interview With Scottish Screen Writer Alan Sharp', RT Burns Club website, (Undated) http://www.rtburnsclub.com/interviews.htm [Accessed 23 Dec 2017].
300 Clouzot, 'Interview with Arthur Penn', 110.

Index

Symbols

6 Rms Riv Vu (Randall-Bower play) 67

20th Century Fox 41, 42, 122

92 in the Shade (McGuane, 1975) 92

A

Actors Studio 9, 81

Adler, Stella 69

Aldrich, Robert 32

Allen, Dede 12, 111, 112, 116, 126

Altman, Robert 4, 22, 131

American Graffiti (Lucas, 1973) 44

Anderson Tapes, The (Lumet, 1971) 81

Apache (Aldrich, 1954) 33

Attica (TV series) (Chomsky, 1980) 136

B

Bainbridge, Beryl 15, 126

Ballad of Cable Hogue, The (Pekinpah, 1970) 97

Barretto, Ray 115

Beatty, Warren 9, 13, 113, 116

Bedford Stuyvesant Restoration Foundation 68

Big Sleep, The (Chandler novel) 51, 58

Big Sleep, The (Hawks, 1946) 45

Binns, Edward 70, 83, 103

Blaustein, Julian 25

Bogart, Humphrey 1, 14, 17, 28, 39, 44, 95

Bogdanovich, Peter 44, 48

Boorman, John 27

Boucher, Le (Chabrol, 1969) 81

Brackett, Leigh 45

Brando, Marlon 9, 11, 12, 135

Breezy (Eastwood, 1973) 55

British Broadcasting Corporation (BBC) 15

Browning, Robert 42, 56

Bruce, Lenny 22

Bruckheimer, Bonnie 43

Burden, Amanda and Carter 68

C

Caine, Michael 15

Canby, Vincent 131

Casablanca (Curtiz, 1942) 18

Chabrol, Claude 81

Chandler (Magwood, 1971) 45

Chandler, Raymond 46, 50, 54, 79

Chappaquiddick 62

Chateau Marmont 41, 79

Chavez, Cesar 68

Chinatown (Polanski, 1974) 4, 45, 116

Clark, Susan 72, 79, 87, 90, 131

Clift, Montgomery 66

CMA Talent Agency 42
Colón, Willie 115
Conversation, The (Coppola, 1974) 66, 72
Coppola, Francis Ford 66, 72, 136
Costello, Anthony 90
Cowboys, The (Rydell, 1972) 42
Crawford, John 99, 109
Crumb, Robert 22
Cruz, Celia 115
Custer, George Armstrong 22

D

Danson, Ted 137
Days of Wine and Roses (Edwards, 1962) 9
Dean, James 11, 44, 66
Death of Billy the Kid (Vidal TV play) (1955) 9
DeHaven III, Carter 25
De Niro, Robert 67
Deray, Jacques 30
Drowning Pool, The (Rosenberg, 1975) 131, 132
Dunaway, Faye 13

E

Eastwood, Clint 55, 69
Easy Rider (Hopper, 1969) 26
Ebert, Roger 131
Ellis, Don 115
Englehardt, Dean 107, 142
Exorcist, The (Friedkin, 1973) 70

F

Fail Safe (Lumet, 1964) 81
Farewell, My Lovely (Richards, 1975) 132
Filmex '75 festival 127
Five Easy Pieces (Rafelson, 1970) 22
Florida Keys 3, 20, 47, 60, 92, 93, 114
Fonda, Peter 22, 26, 49
Ford, John 10, 33
Fort Apache (Ford, 1948) 33
Frankenheimer, John 9, 12, 49, 132
French Connection II, The (Frankenheimer, 1975) 132
French Connection, The (Friedkin, 1971) 58, 66
French New Wave 11, 81

G

Garner, James 45, 67, 69
Gibson, William 12
Godfather Part II, The (Coppola, 1974) 72
Goldsmith, Jerry 115
Gould, Elliot 22
Green Berets, The (Wayne & Kellogg, 1968) 22
Greenock 15, 16, 17, 24, 41, 51
Griffith, Melanie 69, 93, 102, 107, 113, 127, 132
Grusin, Dave 115
Gumshoe (Frears, 1971) 44
Guthrie, Arlo 22

H

Hackman, Gene 3, 7, 42, 58, 67, 69, 70, 73, 83, 89, 92, 97, 99, 103, 109, 131, 132, 137
Hammett, Dashiell 44, 54
Harper (Smight, 1966) 132
Hayworth, Rita 40

Hedren, Tippi 69, 107, 129, 152
Heinman, Laurie 55
Hemingway, Ernest 28, 40, 103
Hepburn, Katharine 14
Hicks, Chuck 109
H.M.S. Victorious 105
Hoffman, Dustin 9, 22
Holden, William 55
Hopper, Dennis 22, 26
Huston, John 1, 18, 30, 39, 58
Huston, John, films directed by
    African Queen, The (1951) 14, 29
    Fat City (1972) 30
    Key Largo (1948) 1, 17, 28, 91, 93, 103
    Maltese Falcon, The (1941) 45
    Treasure of the Sierra Madre, The (1948) 39, 58
    Under the Volcano (1984) 29
    Unforgiven, The (1960) 58
Huston, Tony 29
In the Heat of the Night (Jewison, 1967), 19

I

Indian Dunes Ranch 91

J

Jaws (Spielberg, 1975) 4
Jenkins, George 83
Jeremiah Johnson (Pollack, 1972) 42
Johnson, Don 70
Jones, L. Q. 26

K

Kennedy, Edward 61
Kennedy, John F. 20, 32, 60, 99, 107
Kennedy, Robert F. 18, 20, 32, 60, 68, 69, 100
Kidder, Margot 49, 137
King, Dr. Martin Luther 18
King Lear, 42
Klute (Pakula, 1971) 114
Kopechne, Mary Jo 61
Kotcheff, Ted 35
Kubrick, Stanley 48

L

Lady Chatterley's Lover (Lawrence novel) 17
Lamm, Karen 70
Lancaster, Burt 12, 33, 35, 69, 70, 137
Lasko, Gene 49, 68
Last Picture Show, The (Bogdanovich, 1971) 44
Lavoe, Hector 115
Layton Productions 48
Lemmon, Jack 55
Lenz, Kay 55
Leshansky, Larry 127
Lifton, Mitchell 26
Little Big Man (Berger novel) 23
Little Sister, The (Chandler novel) 45
Long Goodbye, The (Altman, 1973) 4, 45, 132
Los Angeles Memorial Coliseum 83
Lowry, Malcolm 24, 29
Lumet, Sidney 9, 81

M

Macbeth 51
MacDonald, Ross 79

Magnolia Theatre 79
Mailer, Norman 22
Mainwaring, Daniel 43
Major Dundee (Peckinpah, 1965) 33
Malibu 21, 80
Malick, Terrence 113, 116
Manchette, Jean-Patrick 30
Mann, Anthony 10
Marlowe (Bogart, 1969) 45
Marshall, Noel 70
Mars, Kenneth 70, 83, 86
Martin, Strother 26
Marty (Mann, 1955) 9
M*A*S*H (Altman, 1970) 22
McGuane, Thomas 1, 22, 49, 92, 135
McShane, Ian 15
Medavoy, Mike 135
Melville, Jean-Pierre 30
Michaels, Leonard 22
Midnight Man, The (Lancaster, 1974) 70
Mitchum, Robert 132
Monroe, Marilyn 44
Moritz, Bruno 51, 122
Mussante, Tony 29
My Lai massacre 23, 35
My Night At Maud's (Rohmer, 1969) 81
Myra Breckinridge (Sarne, 1970) 41

N

Nashville (Altman, 1975) 131
Native Americans 10, 23, 25, 33, 35
Newman, Paul 9, 11, 66, 132
New Mexico 20, 27, 41, 47, 59, 90, 91, 115, 120
Nichols, Mike 116
Nicholson, Jack 9, 22, 116, 135
Ninety-Two in the Shade (McGuane novel) 92
Nixon, Richard 22, 32, 35, 130
North By Northwest (Hitchcock, 1959) 103

O

Oates, Warren 27, 45, 49
Osterman Weekend, The (Peckinpah, 1983) 136
Oswald, Lee Harvey 62
Othello 56
Out of the Past (Tourneur, 1947) 43

P

Pacino, Al 42
Pakula, Alan J. 114
Pando Productions 27
Parallax View, The (Pakula, 1974) 114
Parton, Dolly 115
Paula (inspiration for character) 3, 20, 40, 57, 61, 72, 133
Peck, Gregory 35
Peckinpah, Sam 26, 33, 97
Penguin Books 16
Penn, Arthur, films directed by
   Alice's Restaurant (1969) 22
   Bonnie and Clyde (1967) 13, 19, 21, 50, 66, 111
   Chase, The (1966) 12, 62
   Four Friends (1981) 136
   Left-Handed Gun, The (1958) 11

Little Big Man (1970) 21, 23, 31, 33, 35
Mickey One (1965) 12, 83
Miracle Worker, The (1962) 12
Missouri Breaks, The (1976) 135, 136, 137
Target (1985) 137
Visions of Eight (1973) 31
Penn, Arthur, plays directed by
　Miracle Worker, The (1959) 83
　Sly Fox (1976) 136
　Two for the Seesaw (1959) 83
Penn, Arthur, TV plays directed by
　"Golden Age of Television" 19
　Miracle Worker, The (1957) 12
Penn, Irving 8
Penn, Matthew 31, 32, 49, 107
Penn, Molly 31, 107
Playboy magazine 85
Play It Again, Sam (Allen play) 44
Point Blank (Boorman, 1967) 27
Polanski, Roman 45
Pollack, Sydney 42, 48
Poseidon Adventure, The (Neame, 1972) 66, 97
Prime Cut (Ritchie, 1972) 66

R

Rafelson, Bob 22, 116, 136
Reagan, Ronald 136
Rebel Without a Cause (Ray, 1955) 11
Redford, Robert 69
Requiem for a Heavyweight (Nelson, 1962) 9
Richards, Emil 115

Rohmer, Eric 79
Roscoe, Sergio 93
Roth, Philip 22
Rotter, Steven A. 112
Royal Academy of Dramatic Art 69
Ruby, Jack 62
Russell, J. D. 105
Rydell, Mark 42, 48

S

Sam's Song (Leondopoulos, 1969) 67
Sanford Productions 42, 48
Sanibel Island 92, 95, 102, 109
Sanibel Moorings (hotel) 93
Save The Tiger (Avildsen, 1973) 55
Scarecrow 42, 66
Schaffner, Franklin J 9
Schatzberg, Jerry 42, 136
Scheider, Roy 132
Schickel, Richard 131
Schifrin, Lalo 115
Schwab's Drugstore 79
Scott, George C. 28, 30, 34
Searchers, The (Ford, 1956) 10
Second Man, The (Behrman play) 69
Sharp, Alan, novels written by
　Apple Pickers, The (unpublished) 23
　Green Tree in Gedde (1965) 16, 71, 90
　Hired Hand, The (novelization, 1975) 133
　Night Moves (novelization, 1971) 52, 56, 61, 89, 120, 133
　Wind Shifts, The (1967) 16, 95

Sharp, Alan, radio plays written by
    Epitath (1968) 23
    Long-Distance Piano Player, The (1962) 15
Sharp, Alan, screenplays and teleplays written by
    Above the Mountain (unproduced) 135
    Billy Two Hats (Kotcheff, 1974) 26, 35, 51
    Dean Spanley (Fraser, 2008) 137
    Hired Hand, The (Fonda, 1971) 26, 30
    Last Run, The (Fleischer, 1971) 26, 27, 30, 34, 51, 57
    Little Treasure (Sharp, 1985) 40, 137
    Love and Lies (Young, 1989) 137
    Osterman Weekend, The (Peckinpah, 1983) 136
    Rob Roy, (Caton-Jones, 1995) 137
    Tepic in the Morning. See *Little Treasure*
    Ulzana's Raid (Aldrich, 1972) 26, 33
Sharp, Alan, television plays written by
    Funny Noises with their Mouths (1963) 15
    Knight in Tarnished Armour (1965) 15
    Sound from the Sea, A (1970) 23
Sharp, Dan 41
Sharp, Liz 19, 41, 65, 126, 136
Sherman, Robert 8, 43, 49, 66, 78, 88, 89, 116, 118, 127, 129, 135
Simenon, Georges 30
Small, Michael 113, 132, 137

Smile (Ritchie, 1975) 127
Soldier Blue (Nelson, 1970) 22
Spiegel, Sam 12
Spielberg, Steven 4, 132
Stair, Bill 27
Stein, Bob 102
Stella Adler Academy 69
Stevenson, Robert Louis 56
Stewart, James 10, 97
Sting, The (Hill, 1973) 44
Strickland, Gail 68
Surtees, Bruce 78, 81
Swan, Peter 17
Sweet William (Bainbridge novel) 126
Sweet William (Whatham, 1980) 127

T

Time to Die, A (Wicker book) 136
To Have and Have Not (Hawks, 1944) 18, 103
To Have and Have Not (Hemingway novel) 18, 39, 103
Towering Inferno, The (Guillermin, 1974) 122
Towne, Robert 116, 118
Tracy, Spencer 97
Train, The (Frankenheimer, 1963) 12
Twelve Angry Men (Lumet, 1957) 9
Tyrone Guthrie Theater 67

U

UNESCO World Heritage Convention 58
Universal Studios 27, 69
USA Film Festival 127

V

Van Gogh, Vincent 24

Vercomtere, Marcel 107

Vidal, Gore 9, 11

Vietnam War 22, 35, 130

Volpone 136

W

Wagoner, Porter 115

Walker & Co. 17

Ward, Janet 70, 81

Warner Books 133

Warner Bros 4, 11, 18, 42, 48, 71, 78, 79, 92, 97, 100, 116, 122, 131

Warner, Jack 24

Warren, Jennifer 69, 73, 107, 109, 113, 116, 117, 121, 130, 132, 136

Warshow, Robert 10

Watergate 22, 43, 69, 130

Wayne, John 22

Way We Were, The (Pollack, 1973) 44

Wells, Frank 129

Wild Bunch, The (Peckinpah, 1969) 26

Wilder, Glenn 109

Wild One, The (Benedek, 1953) 11

Williamstown Theater Festival, Massachusetts 69

Woods, James 70

Writers Guild of America Strike (1973) 49, 71

Y

Yulin, Harris 70, 81

Z

Zandy's Bride (Troell, 1974) 66

Zappa, Frank 22